HARD LEFT

HARD

ANCHOR BOOKS
DOUBLEDAY
New York   London   Toronto   Sydney   Auckland

TAVIS SMILEY

LEFT

Straight Talk about the Wrongs of the Right

An Anchor Book

PUBLISHED BY DOUBLEDAY

a division of Bantam Doubleday Dell Publishing Group, Inc.
1540 Broadway, New York, New York 10036

Anchor Books, Doubleday, and the portrayal of an anchor are trademarks of
Doubleday, a division of Bantam Doubleday Dell Publishing Group, Inc.

Library of Congress Cataloging-in-Publication Data

Smiley, Tavis, 1964–
Hard left: straight talk about the wrongs of the right
Tavis Smiley.
    p. cm.
1. Conservatism—United States. 2. Liberalism—United States.
3. United States—Race relations. 4. United States—
Politics and government—1993– I. Title.
JC573.2.U6S64 1996
320.5′2′097309049—dc20   96-460
CIP

ISBN 0-385-48404-6
Printed in the United States of America
First Anchor Books Edition: June 1996

10 9 8 7 6 5 4 3 2

For my mother, Joyce Marie Smiley,
and
my abiding friend, Harold Patrick,

and in memory of

Jesse A. Brewer,
Earl R. Claiborne, M.D.,
Bishop Robert W. McMurray,
Debra J. Rossiter

Acknowledgments

I have always believed that the three things in life that matter most are faith, family, and friends. Throughout the writing of this book, my faith has sustained me, my family has supported me, and my friends have more than tolerated me.

Because I would be roped and quartered if I failed to mention my nine siblings by name, here goes: Pam, Phyllis, Garnell, Paul, Patrick, Maury, Derwin, Weldon, and Trenton. I love you.

I recognize that I have been blessed beyond measure, and I thank God daily for all things. Including helpful encouragement and guidance from my literary agent, Mel Berger.

Roger Scholl, my editor at Anchor Books, is simply the best. I don't know if or when I will write another book, but I cannot imagine doing so without Roger and his able assistant, Papatya Bucak, who I absolutely adore.

My mother taught me to always pray that those with whom I work will find favor with me. Well, Mother, the respect, kindness, and support I have received from the team at Doubleday has at times overwhelmed me. From Day One, I was treated like a member of their family.

Heartfelt thanks to Madam President Arlene Friedman; to Martha Levin for rolling the dice; to Janet Hill just for being there; to Mario Pulice for a cover design that deserves to win some awards; to Gail Browning for her excitement and enthusiasm; to Ellen Sinkinson for her direction and devotion; to Ellen Archer for her creative suggestions; to Paola Fernandez-Rana for being so affable to work with and for turning me on to her husband's eatery, Mad Fish; to Jayne Schorn for giving this book a real chance; to Charlie Conrad for good conversation and great ideas; and to Emma Bolton, whose pleasant demeanor, hugs, kisses, and candy dish always made my working visits to the office seem like trips to Disneyland!

Many thanks to special friends who in big ways and little have helped to make this book possible, and have made my work more enjoyable and rewarding: Andrea D. Adair, Chi Blackburn, David Brand, Tracey L. Brown, Eula Collins, Dermot D. Givens, Jefferson Graham, Matthew Greene, Pastor Noel N. Jones, Michael Lyles, Marvelous Mack, Sylvester Monroe, Bea Patrick, Denise Pines, Aubrey "Pop" Prince, Bill Reed, Curtis E. Rossiter, Gerald E. Williams, and Daniel Zingale.

Finally, to my remaining dear friends and colleagues who the typesetter would not permit me to mention by name, thank you.

Contents

Introduction

In December 1994, *Time* magazine came out with their roster of America's most promising leaders under the age of forty, something they do every twenty years. In fact, in their 1974 issue, a young promising politician named William Jefferson Clinton made the list. And in 1994, I was one of the "50 for the Future."

"In the wildly popular and largely conservative medium of talk radio, a young black man unafraid to take on the white Establishment would not seem to have a promising future," said *Time*. "But Tavis Smiley, self-styled 'practical progressive,' is making a name for himself—in part because he is equally willing to admonish fellow African Americans who too quickly blame racism for their problems."

A funny thing about the *Time* article. Although I was humbled and honored to have been selected by *Time*'s editors, I couldn't help but notice that the most notable of the young political leaders being profiled were all from the Right, people like Ralph Reed of the Christian Coalition, Republican pollster and strategist Frank Luntz, Congresswoman Susan Molinari, and

Congressman Jim Nussle. Obviously, not one of them is even close to being left of center.

I looked at that and felt something was wrong. I know there are a lot of people on the Left who feel the way I do, but for whatever reason, we're not being heard. Maybe we haven't been speaking loudly enough. Well, we'd better raise our voices quickly before the rhetoric from the Right overwhelms us all.

It's not that the country has gone conservative, it's that those of us who are left of center have allowed the Right to take control of the dialogue. In many respects, we've sat back and allowed this to happen. The great educator Dr. Benjamin E. Mays once said, "He who starts behind in the great race of life must forever remain behind or run faster than the man in front."

I couldn't agree more. Clearly, we are behind in the race. It's time we picked up the pace.

I joined the race in 1964, born in Gulfport, Mississippi, during the height of the civil rights movement. When I was two years old, my father was transferred to Grissom Air Force Base in Bunker Hill, Indiana. Ours was a typical Midwestern small-town life, except for one thing. Indiana had been home to the national headquarters of the Ku Klux Klan, and we never forgot it.

We were poor, ten kids and three adults (Mom, Dad, and my grandmother) sharing a mobile home in a trailer park. We were raised in the church—literally—attending some service or another almost every day of the week. But our faithfulness paid off. While we never had a lot of what we wanted, I can't say we ever went hungry, either.

I grew up as one of a handful of Black kids in an all-

White area. My high school had over a thousand students—and only about twenty-five of them were Black. But although I lived in a nearly all-White community, I never felt "less than" simply because of the color of my skin. I learned that people of different races can and do get along. Which says to me that we don't have to buy this race-baiting, divide-and-conquer technique the radical Right is pushing. I was class president in high school, voted "most likely to succeed," and to this day remain in contact with many of my White high school teachers, who remain friends.

At the age of thirteen, I met former U.S. Senator Birch Bayh of Indiana and got permanently bitten by the political bug. The senator had stopped to campaign at the American Legion in Kokomo. Listening to him that night, I realized the awesome power and potential to motivate people that great politicians have. They have the ability to affect the lives of so many people. It wasn't anything in particular that Senator Bayh said to me that night that changed my life. It was simply his taking the time after his speech to talk to and be photographed with a poor young Black kid, making me feel important and better about my life and my potential for the future.

My dreams of wanting to be a first baseman in the major leagues went out the window that night. I made a vow to God that if I ever got the chance to go to college (no one in my family had ever attended), I would make something of myself and spend the rest of my life trying to positively affect the lives of people who grew up poor: politically, economically, and socially disenfranchised.

At Indiana University, I went all out to become a superachiever. I was a member of the debate team, was actively involved in student government, and worked for the chancellor and vice president of the university, as well as for the mayor of Bloomington. All by the end of my junior year.

But what I really wanted to do was work with Los Angeles Mayor Tom Bradley, the most high-profile Black mayor in America. So I wrote him a letter. And another. And another. I wrote him every day for six months, asking to intern on his staff. I was convinced he was going to be the nation's first elected Black governor (an honor that eventually went to L. Douglas Wilder of Virginia).

All those letters and phone calls eventually got me an appointment to meet with the mayor (who would normally be more inclined to open up spots for young constituents from USC and UCLA), and I not only got the position, but at the end of my internship, I was told by Mayor Bradley that a job would be waiting for me after my graduation.

I worked for the mayor for three years, became the youngest member of his executive staff at the age of twenty-four, and was the mayor's eyes and ears in South Central L.A. I learned the community, the ins and outs of South L.A., and eventually decided to run for City Council at the age of twenty-six.

In the election, I came in fourth in a field of fifteen candidates, and woke up the next morning without a clue about what to do next. I realized that I was most fulfilled when I was helping educate, empower, and encourage people who live and work in the indigenous community. I knew I wanted to run for office again in four years; I needed to find a job that would keep my name in front of the public, would allow me to talk about the issues, and would pay me a salary. It's for that very reason that so many out-of-work politicians turn to hosting talk shows. It's a high-profile job that allows you to say whatever you want—and keep in constant contact with the public.

It was obvious that talk radio was the vehicle for me. I had garnered a lot of votes, so people obviously agreed with what I had to say. And in the melting pot of Los Angeles, there wasn't a single African American commentator on radio or television.

In time, I found a sponsor for my sixty-second radio commentary, "The Smiley Report," and found a home on a small Black-owned radio station, KGFJ. The response was overwhelming. It wasn't that I was a genius—I was just preaching to the choir. I was on Black radio talking about issues I was passionate about, that were vitally important to the renewal of the community, issues our listeners were interested in. Issues like Rodney King, urban redevelopment, and economic opportunity.

"The Smiley Report" eventually became syndicated, and from that one small station, I graduated to bigger radio stations in Los Angeles, as well as KABC-TV, the number one station for news in Southern California. At the age of twenty-seven, I was the lone Black commentator in a field that also included former U.S. Senator John Tunney, prominent L.A. attorney Gloria Allred, and two-time GOP U.S. Senate candidate Bruce Herschensohn.

I once went on the air and blasted Kathleen Brown, who was running for governor of California, for having taken the Black vote for granted. Her record of hiring Black staffers as California treasurer and for awarding jobs to Black-owned firms was abysmal. Shortly thereafter, I received a fax from her office announcing a $500 million state bond being underwritten by a Black-owned company. Not bad for sixty seconds of airtime!

Another time I went after a Black California assemblyman named Curtis Tucker, who had become a pawn of the tobacco industry and was sponsoring a measure to overturn an antismoking bill that had recently passed.

"Doesn't Mr. Tucker know that the fastest-growing group of new smokers today are young Black women?" I asked on the air. "Has Mr. Tucker lost his mind?"

A few days later I got a letter from Mr. Tucker's office telling me that he had dropped the bill.

People always ask me if I intend to run for office again someday. Perhaps. But I've come to realize that the real power in this country today is in the media. You can arguably do more with one sixty-second commentary than with several bills.

Let's see what I can do with a book.

HARD LEFT

1

The Half-Right

On November 8, 1994, America took a sharp right turn away from the principle of life, liberty, and the pursuit of happiness for all its citizens and headed down a misguided and mean-spirited path.

Orchestrated by a small but determined group of right-wing ideologues, a so-called Republican Revolution swept more moderate and progressive thinkers out of Washington and state capitals from California to the Carolinas.

In the wake of this tidal wave of conservative Republicanism, the majority of Americans seem to have simply surrendered. Now, like General Cornwallis at Yorktown, they sing a whiny chorus of "The World Turned Upside Down."

In many ways, the world *has* been turned on its head. In the richest and most powerful nation on the planet, the gap between rich and poor grows ever wider. Fewer and fewer Americans are confident of realizing the American dream, and in an ocean of plenty, everyone from Congress to county governments and corporate CEOs to college students is having trouble making ends meet. In a nation of immigrants, "immigration" has now become a dirty word. Instead of coming together and seeking common solutions to common problems, Black and White Americans, separated by ignorance, fear, and hatred, are moving farther apart.

There is plenty of blame to go around. But ultraconservative Republicans, beginning with the election of Ronald Reagan in 1980, have deliberately played to the current climate of fear and paranoia among White Americans to gain political power, making intolerance, self-interest, and mean-spiritedness the common coin of the realm.

After more than forty years of social and civil rights progress, a Republican political majority now intends to reverse many of those gains by reducing health care for the elderly and infirm, abolishing affirmative action, dismantling welfare, overturning environmental laws, and leaving middle-class Americans without adequate funds for education and community services, while forcing the poor and disadvantaged to fend for themselves in soup kitchens and orphanages.

From the soaring optimism of FDR's New Deal and LBJ's Great Society, we have fallen headlong into the quintessential despair at the heart of the conservatives' Contract with America, undermining America's social contract and recreating a society of a few "haves" and a great many "have-nots."

It doesn't have to be this way. While the GOP controls both houses of Congress and, for the first time in its history, a majority of state houses and legislatures, there are far more registered Democrats in the United States than Republicans. To set things straight again, those who believe the country is headed in the wrong direction must stand up and speak out boldly and clearly against the new Republicans' ill-conceived conservatism. We must tell the self-righteous, right-wing ideologues dominating the Republican party that we are sick and tired of their divisive, race-based politics and their attempt to legislate morality. We must expose what I call the "Contract *on* America"—sold as a Republican alternative to the gridlock of a Democrat-controlled Congress—as an attempt to move the country not forward but lurching dangerously to the conservative right.

I feel the problems facing our country today are much too complex to be solved by any one political ideology. We need the ideas and energy of the best and brightest of all our people, from the Right and the Left. Conservatives force an unofficial litmus test on their leaders, threatening to withdraw support for anyone who doesn't follow the dictates of the conservative agenda. That kind of litmus test and rigid agenda in the end is as paralyzing as the inertia that has enveloped Washington over the last decade.

The fact is, the Right's radical rhetoric and "Take no prisoners" approach to public policy has helped to create a climate of intolerance and hatred, a climate of nastiness and political vigilantism in America, the consequences of which are certain to be grave and catastrophic. The environment of bigotry and intolerance fostered by the Right provides a kind of warped justification for religious and political zealots to right the wrongs of society by taking matters into their own hands. The murdering of doctors at health clinics that perform legal abortions and the bombing of federal buildings by antigovernment fanatics are just the tip of the iceberg, I fear.

The Right would have us believe that much of the violence, sex, and values that appear on television, in the movies, and in music is having a negative influence on our children and an injurious effect on American society at large. That may be true. The irony is, however, that the intolerant rhetoric and the political extremism of the Right has had an equally harmful impact on civil discourse and reasoned debate.

You can't convince me that repeatedly referring to liberal women as "femi-nazis"; labeling those who are "pro-choice" as the "pro-abortion" forces; encouraging radio audiences to shoot federal agents; and holding up Susan Smith's drowning of her two sons in South Carolina as a reason Americans should vote Republican does not have a profoundly negative impact on the levelheadedness of the debate.

Israelis will tell you that one of the reasons Prime

Minister Yitzhak Rabin was assassinated was due to the extremist political language that heightened Israeli passions and exacerbated an already volatile political climate.

In America, we know all too well the results of intolerance and extremism. It's time to check the language, the intolerance, and the mean-spiritedness of the Right before it's too late.

If you break down the conservative agenda, point by point, issue by issue, the net result is backward motion. Outlaw abortion. Repeal affirmative action. Eliminate the National Endowment for the Arts. Discriminate against gays and lesbians. Close our borders. Cut Medicare.

I call conservatives the Half-Right, because they only tell you half the story. But let me surprise you for a moment by telling you what I *like* about the Right. When they talk about the moral fabric of our country being torn apart and the need for a return to family values, they are right. I admire their organizational skills: walking precincts, fund-raising, organizing letter-writing and phone-in campaigns, and getting out the vote. They mobilize the troops and stay focused on their issues.

What I don't like are the half-truths they espouse like Holy Writ from on high. What's wrong with their movement can be summed up by the three D's:

DISTORTION, DECEPTION, AND DOGMATISM

They **distort** the truth to further their half-baked agenda to move the country to the right. But you can't move forward by going backward. They **deceive** us by assuring that they have our interests—the interests of the American public—at heart. They know full well that they have only the interests of like-minded conservatives at heart, those who believe we all must accept their way, and *only* their way. And God help you if you are Black, Hispanic, Asian, any other person of color, or, worse, gay. Anything *different.*

Their **dogmatism** makes them impervious to any person or position that doesn't agree with their philosophy. There is little room for debate. There can be no compromise. It is their way—or the highway.

DISTORTION

According to a recent voter survey, Americans reject the Christian Coalition's claim that they speak for American families or for people of faith in matters of public policy. While 56 percent of Americans consider themselves to be "strongly religious," only 18 percent said the Christian Coalition "speaks for me" on political issues. Sixty-five percent say they worry that groups like the Christian Coalition "go too far in mixing religion with politics" and more than half feel it is inappropriate for the Christian Coalition to claim their political positions are based on "Christian values." From vouchers for private and religious schools to abolishing the Department of Education, from restricting abortion to eliminating federal family planning, Americans oppose the Christian Coalition's agenda by large and decisive margins.

In the affirmative action debate, the Right insists on using two terms to frame the discussion: "quotas" and "racial preferences." The fact is that quotas are illegal unless imposed by a court and have been since the 1978 Bakke case, argued before the Supreme Court. But this hasn't stopped the Right from using such rabid rhetoric, however untrue it is. Additionally, the term "racial preference" suggests that affirmative action policies blindly and artificially hire and promote certain groups over others without regard to qualifications. Not true. Indeed, as the Right well knows, the reason that affirmative action and "set-asides" exist in the first place is because too often qualified applicants are rejected simply on the basis of their race. And it was a Republican, President Richard Nixon, who expanded the affirmative action program in the 1970s and established the use of goals and timetables.

Yet another distortion was perpetrated by conservative commentator and author William F. Buckley, Jr., when he wrote in 1993 that: "The vast majority of the people Blacks kill are other than Blacks.'' Yet, 80 percent of murdered Whites were killed by other White Americans. The truth is that most criminals kill their own kind. Three-quarters of White victims of violent crime say their attacker was White; well over 85 percent of African American victims say their attacker was Black. Although crime is a serious problem in America, and in the Black community especially, the leading factor in the rise of minority incarcerations has been the change in our drug policies, not an increase in crime, according to a 1995 report from The Sentencing Project, a nonprofit research and advocacy organization in Washington. African Americans, for example, constitute 13 percent of monthly drug users, but represent 35 percent of arrests for drug possession, 55 percent of convictions, and 74 percent of prison sentences.

Robert L. Bartley, editor of the nation's most conservative newspaper, *The Wall Street Journal,* argued in his book about the Reagan years, *The Seven Fat Years: And How to Do It Again,* that the 1980s were a time of great prosperity, compared to Jimmy Carter's term. Bartley claimed the nation grew by 3.8 percent under Reagan, compared to Carter's 1.6 percent. But that's another distortion. According to FAIR (Fairness and Accuracy in Reporting), Bartley's methodology was skewed: ''This fundamentally dishonest comparison assigns two recessions—only one of which occurred even partially during his presidency—to Carter, while counting no recessions for Reagan. You could find a 3.5 percent growth rate for Carter by playing a similar game and counting from 1975 to 1980.''

Numbers don't lie. But they do distort.

DECEPTION

The Right not only distorts the truth, they also use outright deception to mislead the American public. Here are just a few outrageous deceptions perpetrated by the Right.

The Motor Voter Bill

When Congress debated and eventually passed the bill that allowed people in all fifty states to register to vote while applying for or renewing their driver's license, most Republicans argued against the bill, saying it would lead to greater voter fraud. That was pure deception. In truth, Republicans were against it because they feared the majority of new voters would register as Democrats, and as a result, ultimately benefit the Left far more than it would the Right. Clearly, it wasn't to their advantage to have an increase in voter registration, despite their trumpeting the principle of democracy and their claim to speak for the American people. The fact is that Republicans didn't win back control of Congress in 1994 by signing up new voters; they just motivated the faithful to get to the polls. By the way, in the first eight months after the motor voter bill went into effect, more than 5 million people were added to voter registration rolls and most of the new registrants listed themselves as independents.

Welfare

The Right claims that welfare is ruining the nation's economy. This is hogwash and they know it. But the poor are an easy group to pick on, because they contribute little money to political campaigns. The truth is that welfare accounts for less than 1 percent of the national deficit. If we abolished "welfare as we know it" tomorrow, it wouldn't make a dent in the national deficit. And there are other forms of government welfare the Right shies away from, like subsidies for farmers and ranchers. The Half-Right encourages the implication that welfare is synonymous with single Black mothers. Once again, it's simply not true. The majority of people on welfare are White women. Finally, the Right claims that welfare becomes a way of life for most recipients. The truth is that most welfare dependents are on and off the system within two years. Those who return to welfare do so not because they're lazy, don't want to work, or wish to scam the system, but because they can't afford to pay rent and raise kids on a minimum wage salary.

Three Strikes

The "three strikes" law—which locks up criminals for life after the third felony—has been touted by conservatives as the solution to the increase in violent crime in America. Unfortunately, as conservatives know, it has backfired. Because a guilty plea now means twenty-five years to a life term, more defendants prefer to take their chances before a jury rather than plea-bargain. As a result, criminal trials have multiplied and lengthened, further backlogging the already taxed criminal court system. Worse, we're overcrowding our prisons. The California Department of Corrections projects that today's prison population of 128,000 will grow to more than 210,000 by the year 2000—an increase of more than 15,000 inmates per year. We have nowhere to house them even now. To make room, guess who is often being let out? Child molesters, muggers, thieves, and rapists. And some of the folks being locked away for decades for their third offense were convicted of relatively minor and nonviolent crimes, like stealing a pizza or, even worse, four cookies. Crime is a genuine concern for all Americans. Simple solutions that don't address the realities of the problem are merely political expediency.

Gay Rights

One of the more brilliant deceptions proliferated by the Right is the argument against so-called "special rights" or "privileges" for gay Americans. The fact is that no one in the gay community that I know of is asking for special rights. What they do want and deserve, quite frankly, are basic legal protections against discrimination in housing, employment, and public accommodations. The Right continues to frame the debate about gays and lesbians in terms of "special privileges" in an attempt to legislate morality. I'm still not convinced that we can legislate morality. But I am thoroughly convinced that we can regulate behavior. Many from both the Right and the Left will never condone same-sex relationships. Fine. But we must all agree to protect the rights of any and every American from unfair discrimination based solely on one's race, color, creed, religion, gender, or sexual orientation.

Environment

From Teddy Roosevelt to Richard Nixon, Republicans embraced the notion of protecting and preserving our environment. Indeed, it was Nixon who extended federal protection to water, air, and endangered animals and plants. The Right *says* it is still environment-friendly, but believes that rewards, rather than regulations, encourage people to take care of the environment. "Rewards, not regulations"—where have we heard that deception before?

In truth, with the Reagan Administration came an assault on environmental laws and the federal agencies that enforce them, from Reagan's comment "When you've seen one redwood, you've seen them all" to that of his Secretary of the Interior, James Watt, who once likened environmentalism to Nazism.

Now that they control Congress, Newt and the Fanatics have picked up where Reagan left off, setting out to destroy the Environmental Protection Agency (EPA) by slashing its budget 34 percent and speeding up efforts to wipe out the nation's wetlands and open up wildlife refuges, wilderness areas, and even national parks to oil drilling, mining, and other commercial development.

But even big business has balked at some of the

GOP's radical and regressive proposals. Speaking to *The Los Angeles Times,* chemical industry executive and former Bush Administration EPA official Linda Fisher questioned the wisdom of gutting the EPA: "EPA's stamp of approval tells the American public that our products are safe to use, and that's fine with us."

Apparently, the only thing "green" the new Right likes is campaign contributions.

DOGMATISM

Dog·ma·tism \n\: a viewpoint or tenet put forth as authoritative without adequate grounds; a system of ideas based on insufficiently examined premises; a principle, belief, or statement of opinion considered to be absolute truth.

Dogmatism

The Right trying to overturn the Brady Bill and the assault weapons ban, keeping handguns and those nasty and needless semiautomatic AK-47s on America's streets. Notice these weapons of mass destruction aren't called hunting weapons—no, they're used to *assault*—to kill ex-wives, current and former employers, children and innocent bystanders at your local post office. In 1994, former presidents Reagan, Ford, and Carter jointly wrote Congress asking for a ban on the killing machines. "Although assault weapons account for less than 1 percent of the guns in circulation, they account for nearly 10 percent of the guns traced to crime," they wrote.

Dogmatism

Blaming the Left for all of society's problems. When Susan Smith drowned her two sons in South Carolina and the nation was looking for answers, House Speaker Newt Gingrich said such crimes could be prevented simply by voting Republican. Worse yet, after Debra Evans, her ten-year-old daughter, and eight-year-old son were kidnapped and murdered—her unborn child being cut from her uterus—Gingrich didn't offer any sympathy to the family; instead he blamed the Left for the "moral decay" and the "welfare state" that led to their deaths.

Dogmatism

Cigarette smoking is the leading cause of preventable death in the nation, yet the Right has publicly embraced tobacco as a personal freedom issue. Gingrich spokesman Tony Blankley calls antismokers "health nazis." We're talking about a legal product that kills half a million people a year, compared to illegal drugs, which claim the lives of three thousand a year. The Right has done everything in their power to cut back on government efforts to put nicotine in its place—as a drug—and to restrict the tobacco companies' campaigns to hook young kids early. Indeed, Philip Morris chairman Geoffrey Bible, in a 1995 letter to shareholders, wrote, "New faces and new leadership on Capitol

Hill mean Philip Morris . . . has tremendous opportunities."

Dogmatism

The attempt to abolish federal support for arts, humanities, and public broadcasting. The Right argues that such funding is a waste of taxpayers' dollars because: "The government now funds controversial and obscene works." In other words, in terms of art, either you espouse our values or no values. Art *is* subjective. Who's to decide what is an acceptable artistic expression? Clearly, government-funded work does more good than harm. PBS provides some of the best nonviolent, educational, and diversified programming for children anywhere. If we really want to help families and teach children good values, as the Right says it does, we should strengthen public television, not weaken it. The National Endowment for the Arts and the National Endowment for the Humanities have been responsible for exposing millions of Americans to art that they might not have otherwise experienced and enjoyed.

Dogmatism

Conservative education activists are determined to push their views and values on us all. They want to dismantle public education in America, for example, by supporting school voucher proposals, funneling money to private schools, and by dictating what can and cannot be taught in public schools. In school districts across the country, right-wing fundamentalists are attempting to take control of school boards through local elections and force schools to incorporate creationism and school prayer into the curriculum, while filibustering about sex education, birth control, and homosexuality.

Shall I continue? The "We are right, they are wrong" dogma, which the Right spews out almost daily, speaks to the sexism, racism, and intolerance that characterizes too much of the conservative agenda.

ON BLACK CONSERVATIVES

Before I move on to talk about what we, the Left, must do to turn the tide against the extreme Right, I feel that as a Black commentator, I would be remiss if I did not offer a few words on so-called Black conservatives.

Gaddy Vasquez, the first Latino president of the Orange County Board of Supervisors in California, in a speech at the Republican National Convention in 1988, derided Democratic candidate Governor Michael Dukakis by saying, "He may speak Spanish, but he doesn't speak our language."

That's exactly how I feel about Black conservatives. They're of my color but not my kind. Isn't the phrase "Black conservative" an oxymoron anyway? I've often wondered what it is these Black Americans are conserving.

The Right isn't just Newt Gingrich and Pat Robertson. Part of the front line of the attack on the Left includes Supreme Court Justice Clarence Thomas, radio talk-show hosts Ken Hamblin and Armstrong Williams, professors Shelby Steele and Walter Williams, economist Thomas Sowell, and congressmen Gary Franks of Connecticut and J. C. Watts of Oklahoma, to name a few. Like the Black soldiers in the film *Glory*, these Black conservatives have been pushed to the front of an armed charge to retake the hills upon which America was built. The only problem is that it is not an America that was available to or open to Blacks.

In 1995 a protest march organized by Black leaders took place in front of the home of Clarence Thomas to express the Black community's disapproval over his attacks on practically everything and everyone that is Black. Clarence Thomas is Black America's worst nightmare; neither he nor other Black conservatives speak for Black America. Conservative Blacks have been anointed by the Right Establishment, rather than elected by anyone in the Black community, for reasons that are mostly because of their pigmentation and only to a small degree because of their argumentation. The Right's very promotion of Black conservatives is an enormous act of duplicity and deception.

The truth is that of the thirty-eight Black members of Congress (two seats are presently vacant), only *two* are conservatives, Franks and Watts. Not surprisingly, they have been elected from predominantly White districts, which suggests to me that if you're a Black conservative in this country, you can't be elected to dogcatcher within the Black community. I welcome the debate in the coming months and years about the new Black conservatism. But unless and until these modern-day conservatives can fill more than a small telephone booth with their Black constituency, I wouldn't believe the hype behind their supposed mandate or following.

Too much of right-wing politics is aimed squarely against Black Americans and other minorities. Unfortunately, like slavery itself, many of the advances of present-day conservatives could not have been accomplished without help from the ranks of those being victimized.

Just as Africans aided slave traders in the search and capture of other Africans—wittingly or otherwise—Black conservatives have aided and abetted efforts to roll back many of the hard-won social, economic, and political gains among the African American community over the past forty years.

By endorsing the half-truths and distortions of conservative Whites for ending affirmative action or cutting welfare, Black conservatives have allowed themselves to be used to carry out the dirty work of close-minded people who do not have the interests of African Americans and poor people at heart. Worse, they lend credibility to views that are misguided and often racist.

Although he stands little chance of winning the 1996 Republican presidential nomination, the campaign of Black conservative Alan Keyes and the publication of such books as *Made in America* by Ken Hamblin and *Beyond Blame: How We Can Succeed by Breaking the Dependency Barrier* by Armstrong Williams will undoubtedly add to the hoopla surrounding Black conservatives. One almost gets the impression that African Americans are becoming a bunch of right-wingers. Yet every poll, study, and survey in America shows that the overwhelming majority of Black Americans believe, for example, that affirmative action is fair, remedies a historic injustice, and allows for the admission, hiring, or promoting of *all* qualified candidates. They also oppose school choice, fearful that it will further ruin inner-city schools; oppose three strikes legislation, not because they are soft on crime but because they believe in second chances; oppose the death penalty, not because they don't want to punish criminals but because they are aware of how unfair the system can be; and support a more expansive view of government.

The debate between Black liberals and Black conservatives dates back at least as far as W. E. B. Du Bois and Booker T. Washington, who had profound disagreements on the direction of social, political, and economic policy for Black Americans at the beginning of this century. However, Du Bois and Washington always had the best interests of Black people at heart. I think many of the Black conservatives today are interested primarily in their own self-promotion and financial gain, rather than in whether or not Black people will suffer. The only thing the Right wants from Black people is a vote—and the help of Black people in condemning those Black stereotypes of which the Right doesn't approve and which the Right blames for the moral decay of America.

When was the last time you heard a Black conservative say anything *positive* about Black people? When was the last time you heard a Black conservative say anything remotely *challenging* to White America? They rarely do, because they know the audience they're playing to—conservative Whites. Why is it that Black conservatives ignore discrimination, as if denying that racism still exists? Why is it that all the prominent Black conservatives are men? Why is it that even the brightest Black conservative minds, people like Black conservative economist Thomas Sowell, or English professor Shelby Steele, frequently comment on race, and yet are almost never quoted in the mainstream media on economic policy or English literature? The Right marginalizes the talents of Black conservatives, even as it solicits their opinions on race matters.

The fact is that Clarence Thomas is on the Supreme Court primarily because he's Black. No objective person can state with a straight face that Clarence Thomas was the best-qualified person to be nominated for the court. But he was a Black federal judge who walked the Right walk and talked the Right talk. So he became Bush's man. Strangely, the Right complains bitterly and often about gender- and race-based politics. Yet, Clarence Thomas was chosen, in large part, because of the Right's very cynicism over issues of race and gender, in much the same way Justice Sandra Day O'Connor was chosen by Ronald Reagan, who wanted to appoint the first woman to sit on the high court. (Although most would agree she's proved herself a very capable judge, few would say she was the best-qualified candidate at the time she was nominated.) Her nomination, in a sense, was a form of affirmative action.

Why are Black conservatives blind publicly to the fact that most Black Americans have always been conservative on moral issues and liberal on social issues? And what's wrong with that, anyway? Blacks are by and large much more conservative than other groups on many of the important moral issues of the day, including the hot-button topics of abortion and school prayer, in part because of the Black communities' deep and abiding religious faith. But do they think of themselves as "conservatives"? No. Because on social issues they have little to conserve.

In the affirmative action debate, a great many people, including Republican Senator Bob Dole, bastardize Dr. Martin Luther King, Jr.'s words that one day he hoped his four little children would "live in a nation where they will not be judged by the color of their skin but by the content of their character." The Half-Right uses this quote to suggest that Dr. King wanted to live in a color-blind society. That is simply not true. Dr. King never believed in or argued for a color-blind society. While he wanted his children and others to be judged by the content of their characters, he did not want to live in a homogenized America. King believed as I do that America's greatest strength is her diversity.

What they conveniently forget is that Dr. King also said this: "When millions of people have been cheated for centuries, restitution is a costly process. Inferior education, poor housing, unemployment, inadequate health care—each is a bitter component of the oppression that has been our heritage. Each will require billions of dollars to correct. Justice so long deferred has accumulated interest and its cost for this society will be substantial in financial as well as human terms. The great majority of Americans are suspended between these opposing attitudes. They are uneasy with injustice but unwilling yet to pay a significant price to eradicate it."

Put simply, Black conservatives are being used by the Right. Indeed, House Speaker Newt Gingrich has an unofficial plan called the GOP Minority Outreach Strategy, which calls for the GOP to "promote" its *six* minority House members—at press conferences, in action on the floor of the House, and through informal TV responses to the President. It advocates finding minorities to testify at congressional hearings and creating a GOP mailing list of minority groups.

Meanwhile, the Right continues to cut programs that have historically helped Black Americans and other persons of color. The earned income tax credit, public housing programs, summer jobs for inner-city youth. How dare they?

This is not about race, it's about reason. It's about where the Right stands on the issues that matter to Black America. These Black mouthpieces and talking heads do not speak for the Black community. Everyone on the Left must counter conservatives who claim or imply that they speak for an entire ethnic group— whatever their race.

The national NAACP shamefully avoided opposing Clarence Thomas's nomination to the Supreme Court because he is a Black man. The nation's oldest and largest civil rights organization refused to criticize a man who could care less about civil rights, simply because he was of the right race. But who benefits from this? Certainly not Black Americans. Ironically, with his back to the wall and his nomination in grave doubt, Clarence Thomas had the audacity to play the race card himself, calling the Senate hearings a "high-tech lynching of a Black man." Clarence Thomas is now a lifetime member of the nation's highest court, and he gleefully gives Black America a swift kick in the behind every chance he gets.

I do not find diversity of thought in the Black community troubling. Indeed, no race is best served by monolithic thinking. There must always be room for reasonable people, regardless of race, to agree to disagree on important issues. What is pure deception, however, is the way a small but well-connected and well-placed group of Black right-wingers can claim to represent the Black vote in America. It just ain't so.

2

Hard Left

Liberals and progressives cannot blame all the problems facing the nation today on conservatives. Sadly, old-line liberalism must shoulder a major share of the blame for allowing the political and social climate to disintegrate to this degree in America.

We must light a fire under those on the Left to overcome the inertia that has plagued liberals for the past two decades. Attacking conservatives is not enough. We must stand up for what we believe, and stop turning away from what we know to be right for ourselves and this country.

During the 1992 presidential campaign, Bill Clinton twisted himself into a pretzel trying to escape the negative tax-and-spend, soft-on-crime connotations now synonymous with liberalism. One got the sense that Clinton didn't want to get too far Left, unable to get back to the center. One distressing example of his rightward march toward "moderate" ground was his political shunning of African Americans. In a strategy to win White male votes, Clinton sought to avoid the kind of "Willie Horton" problem that sank the presidential aspirations of fellow liberal Democrat Michael Dukakis in 1988 by keeping his campaign appearances in the African American community to a bare minimum.

The 1992 campaign was just a taste of what was to come during the early years of the Clinton Administration. Constantly having to prove that he wasn't a tax-and-spend liberal, Clinton moved farther and farther right, compromising many of the programs and policies he supported during his campaign. Instead of passing a health care package, he got bogged down in a race to beat Republicans to the punch on a tax cut that runs counter to deficit reduction. Instead of welfare reform, he was pushed into a review of affirmative action. More than halfway through his tumultuous first term, Clinton spent more time moving right than moving forward on the national agenda.

The shame of it is that we, the Left, have allowed the Right to grossly distort who and what we are. Through our own timidity, we have let others transform the word "liberal"—and everything associated with it—into something undesirable and un-American. We have let them recast fifty years of liberal achievement into a gigantic social misstep that only the Right can correct.

Part of the problem has been our own confusion about the true meaning of liberalism. Somehow those on the Left have harbored the misguided notion that it is impolitic to criticize our leaders and our allies when they are wrong. One of the traps of liberalism has been the fear of offending anyone who shared the label.

Liberals have always bent over backward not to offend the varied special-interest groups who have shared the progressive coalition. Black liberals, for example, have considered criticizing even the most corrupt Black politician to be "airing one's dirty laundry" in public and a betrayal of the Black community. Quite frankly, some people need to be offended. Corrupt politicians, Black or White, deserve to be offended. Americans who do not do all that they can do for themselves and who have become needlessly dependent on government largesse also deserve the criticism of the Left.

When Black conservatives and others lecture African Americans about the need to exercise more self-help and personal responsibility, they are right. But they are only half-right. Self-help and personal responsibility have always been a part of the Black agenda. But to tell people that racism doesn't exist, to ask them to pick themselves up by their bootstraps when they have no boots is not only unrealistic, it is irresponsible.

Government has an obligation to provide equal opportunity for all its citizens through quality public education, freedom from discrimination in employment and housing, and adequate public safety. And when government does not provide these basic rights, then government should be criticized and challenged.

We should be creating coalitions and supporting worthy candidates and causes across ideological lines, presenting a new brand of liberalism with a proactive, progressive approach to solving the nation's problems. That means standing up and not retreating from the traditional liberal principles that made this country great.

In one of his finest moments, during a televised debate toward the end of his 1994 campaign, an embattled Ted Kennedy exhibited precisely the kind of bold passion that every member of the long-dormant progressive coalition must display if we are to avoid extinction.

Fighting for his political life, the liberal Democratic senator launched an angry but heartfelt volley at his conservative Republican opponent, Mitt Romney, who challenged Kennedy's commitment to his Massachusetts constituents. Proudly highlighting a distinguished career of public service and championing the causes of the poor and disadvantaged, Kennedy saved his seat in the U.S. Senate. Democratic senators Jeff Bingaman of New Mexico and Charles Robb of Virginia did the same thing in states that are far less liberal.

That brand of honest indignation is long overdue in the liberal Democratic camp. Instead of running from the label of liberalism, it is time to stand up and say in no uncertain terms that there is nothing wrong with being on the side of the poor and the least among us.

Newt Gingrich and the Right have defined their fight against the Left as a "culture war." I believe firmly that most Americans believe in and share a basic core set of values which we live by daily, regardless of our race, sex, creed, color, or political persuasion. So I would characterize the debate less as a "culture war" than a bitter yet necessary fight for the future and direction of this great country. And in any good fight, nothing counters a sharp right like a hard left.

It is a fight in which the Right seems to be taking no prisoners. Whether we like it or not, the gloves have already come off.

On the heels of the so-called Republican Revolution that swept the country in the November 1994 elections, some have argued that liberalism has played itself out. No less than seven Democrats have already announced that they will not seek reelection to the U.S. Senate.

Clearly, the Republicans are sharpening their knives. Quite honestly, I've seen better odds. But I'm a fighter. That's all I know how to do—fight for what I believe in, whatever the odds against me.

Dr. Martin Luther King, Jr., once said: "Cowardice asks, is it safe? Expediency asks, is it politic? Vanity asks, is it popular? But conscience asks, is it right? There comes a time when one must take the position that is neither safe nor politic nor popular, but he must do it because conscience tells him, it is right."

I believe that practical, progressive liberalism is right for America . . . more so now than ever before. Addressing the Democratic National Convention in San Francisco on July 16, 1984, then-New York Governor Mario Cuomo defined liberalism as follows:

"We believe in only the government we need, but we insist on all the government we need.

"We believe in a government characterized by fairness and reasonableness, a reasonableness that goes beyond labels, that doesn't distort or promise to do what it knows it can't do. A government strong enough to use the words 'love' and 'compassion' and smart enough to convert our noblest aspirations into practical realities.

"We believe that a society as blessed as ours, the most affluent democracy in the world's history, that can spend trillions on instruments of destruction, ought to be able to help the middle class in its struggle, ought to be able to find work for all who can do it, room at the table, shelter for the homeless, care for the elderly and infirm, hope for the destitute.

"We believe in firm but fair law and order, in the union movement, in privacy for people, openness by government, civil rights, and human rights. We believe in a single, fundamental idea that describes better than most textbooks and any speech what a proper government should be. The idea of family. Mutuality. The sharing of benefits and burdens for the good of all. Feeling one another's pain. Sharing one another's blessings. Reasonably, honestly, fairly—without respect to race or sex or geography or political affiliation.

"We believe we must be the family of America, recognizing that at the heart of the matter, we are bound one to another."

Unfortunately, the Democratic party did not put these shining words into effect. They were too mired in the same old tired formulas and social agendas of the past, whether they worked or not. They were unwilling to reinvent government, but only to rephrase its rhetoric. As a result, the party relinquished its position of leadership and fell back before the countermanifesto of the Right.

What can we do to turn the tide? How do we take back the mantle of leadership? I have, perhaps presumptuously, put together what I refer to as my "Top Ten Wish List for the Left," which I'll unveil in a moment. Before I launch into it, let me preface my ideas with a simple warning. I bring no new revelations, no panaceas, no words spoken to me from on high through a burning bush on a mountaintop. But insanity is doing the same thing the same way and expecting a different result.

What I do offer is perhaps a different perspective, and a lot of passion, and what I hope is a fresh approach to some rather stale problems. New energy and a new outlook. Simple yet straight talk. A list of principles which I believe will take us in the right direction. A direction we need to go in—*now*. Yesterday, in fact.

STOP THE SILENCE

I've yet to understand why or how we allowed the Right to foster the notion that they are the only ones who believe in God, devotion to family, law and order, self-reliance, commitment to excellence, rewarding achievement, and bold patriotism. Nonsense.

The irony here is that traditionally the Republican party has been the party of the rich and the lucky. It has been the Democratic party that has always fought for the working class, the disadvantaged, and Americans in the middle—the majority of people in the country. Are we then to believe that Americans who struggle every day to work and raise a family, to go to college, to own a home, and to secure a safe and happy old age shun traditional American values? At one point, my father, to support our family, held down a handful of part-time jobs to augment his income as an Air Force officer. I've never known anyone with a stronger work ethic. But like countless millions, my father is a long, long, long way from the Right. The fact is that most Americans—whatever their race, ideology, gender, region, or religion—believe in these sacred American principles. Conservatives' attempts to claim them as their own is a classic distortion of the Right. The time to stop the silence is now. Those of us who make up the Left, who believe in these old-fashioned American values, must speak up.

COUNTERING DEFECTORS
AND UNIFYING OUR VOICE

After the November 1994 elections, it seemed that almost daily there was yet another announcement by a congressional Democrat that he was changing party affiliation, despite the fact that he had just been elected or reelected as a Democrat, supporting the Democratic platform.

For me, this is a betrayal. These folks ran as Democrats, siphoned Democratic resources, stole our votes, and defected to the party of the elite. It reminds me of that old joke that we're all Democrats until we make a little money. Or in this case, until the Republicans take back both houses of Congress.

Anyone who defected following the Republican takeover should be subject to swift, certain, and severe punishment from those who oppose the conservative Right. They should be specifically targeted for defeat in 1996. They must be made examples of to discourage future subversion of our votes.

We need to unify our voice and our vote. Consider how conservative Republicans responded when Willie Brown, then-California Democratic assembly speaker and now mayor of San Francisco, attempted to transfer his influence and power to a Republican of his choice. After the GOP swept the 1994 California election, Brown, realizing that a Republican would eventually take over his job, cut a deal to deny the post to his archenemy, Republican majority leader Jim Brulte. He did this by announcing his support for Republican Doris Allen, an obscure politician from Orange County. Brown and the Democrats all voted along with Allen to elect her to the position. Republicans were incensed. They retaliated by launching an all-out campaign to undermine her effectiveness.

In California, the speaker appoints all committee chairs and has tremendous authority and power. But when Allen offered plum appointments and assignments to members of her own party, they turned her down. There was virtually no one in the Republican party who would have anything to do with her. Instead, they mounted a recall campaign against Allen in her district. Eventually, she was forced to resign her post as speaker to concentrate on fighting the recall, even though due to term limits, she could not seek reelection beyond 1996, anyway. But the Republicans were hell-bent on making an example out of her. And guess what? She lost by a two-to-one margin.

That's the way the Right reinforces its position within the party.

TOWARD A LESS IDEOLOGICAL AGENDA

If you poll most Americans on the major issues of our time, you're likely to get a lot of agreement. But ask Americans how to solve those problems and the consensus usually ends. There are Republican solutions, Democratic solutions, conservative and neoconservative solutions, liberal and libertarian solutions.

To varying degrees, all offer some insight. But the world and its problems have become increasingly complex. Let's face it. No one political party or ideology has all the answers. And as we approach the next millennium, it has become increasingly clear that twentieth-century ideological labels like "liberal" and "conservative" are too narrow and simplistic for the complex problems confronting us on the dawn of the twenty-first century.

In the early 1960s, John F. Kennedy's Camelot proclaimed the end of ideology. It turned out to be premature. The fact is, however, that it is not necessarily an end of ideology that we need, but rather new, less restricting ideologies that do not always box voters or politicians in by limiting their options and open-mindedness in confronting the problems of the nation today.

Most Americans are more liberal on some issues and more conservative on others. They would prefer to see our country move forward, rather than to the left or to the right.

I believe in the credo articulated by Mario Cuomo at the 1984 Democratic Convention—the belief in a government that encourages the talented but finds room at the table for the middle class, the elderly, and the infirm; that offers hope for the jobless and the homeless. But what we need ideologically is a more practical, progressive approach to problem-solving, rather than one that is predetermined by ideology, whether left or right.

We should not be afraid to admit that welfare is broken and ought to be fixed. While we should not close our eyes to the fact that we have to be more frugal in times of fiscal restraint, that does not mean we cannot have compassion.

Instead of giving in to those who practice a politics of race and repeal, we need to stand up boldly and clearly say that affirmative action is flawed but works, that it would benefit from being reformed but shouldn't be abolished altogether.

We need to make it clear that we are not antiimmigrant, but that our immigration policy needs an overhaul. Yes, some of our social services are overburdened. But we should remember that America's strength is her diversity and that the fomenters of racial fear and hatred undermine that strength.

We need to make clear in no uncertain terms that we are not soft on crime. We insist on a safe and nurturing America. Moreover, let me say that as disproportionate victims of violent crime who sit on juries every day and convict guilty people of all races, African Americans find it particularly offensive when people say that O. J. Simpson went free just because he is Black.

We need to acknowledge that traditional liberalism isn't working. But rather than running away from it, or tossing it into some dustbin of history, we must recast and reshape it anew to fit our changing times and needs. If we do not, we may find ourselves in an America we no longer recognize.

NOT JUST WHAT WE'RE AGAINST— WHAT WE'RE FOR

The Right's Contract with America was dead wrong on almost every one of its agendas. Some elements of the contract were so transparently insincere that a blind person could see through them. Did anyone really believe the Right had any serious intentions of passing a term-limits measure? Think about it. After almost fifty years of being the minority party, they finally take control of both houses of Congress. Did we really believe they would immediately go about legally limiting their stay?

Yeah, right.

I will confess that the Contract with America was a brilliant strategic stroke by the Right. They offered a single document that could be held up to the American people, stating: "This is what we believe. If elected, this is what we are going to do. This is our game plan."

The problem with the Left is that we have not been able to do the same thing. We've argued at every turn what we're against, but what are we for? We know the answer to the welfare problem is *not* orphanages, as House Speaker Newt Gingrich once suggested. We know that the answer to revitalize and restore the educational system in this country is *not* to cut education funding. But what are we advocating?

We need to give the American electorate a clear vision of what we are for, accompanied by a blueprint for construction. The American people are hungry for capable leaders who have a detailed and specific plan of action.

We can only go so far playing defense. It's an important part of the game—ask any football, basketball, or baseball coach. But sooner or later you've got to put some points on the scoreboard. You've got to generate some offense. If both teams play perfect defense, you still have a zero-sum game. It's time for us to score some points.

GET ANGRY

Why did the conservatives come to power with a "decided sense of vengeance," even though the political tide has so clearly turned in their favor? In researching the issue for *GQ* magazine in 1995, writer Joseph Nocera discovered that of the many bitter Beltway battles fought over the past decade, the fight over Supreme Court nominee Robert Bork is the one that still angers conservatives the most.

Conservatives' blood has been boiling ever since, both because the Right had so much riding on this particular nomination—Bork would have become the decisive vote on such controversial and important issues as abortion, school prayer, and affirmative action—and because the Right felt that Bork had been demonized by the Left in an unfair and slanderous smear campaign to keep a conservative off the court. During the nominating battle, *The Wall Street Journal* even coined a new verb: "to Bork," meaning to destroy a nominee by any means necessary.

Immediately following the Bork defeat, suggests Nocera, the Right went ballistic. I think he's right. They have been on the warpath ever since.

The question is: What will it take to fire up the Left in the same way? I don't know what we are waiting for. If affirmative action or welfare isn't the issue, perhaps cutting Medicare and Medicaid is, or the tax cut and capital gains tax reduction for the wealthy paid for by eliminating school lunches for kids.

What's particularly disturbing about our apathy is the fact that we have the numbers to turn the political situation around: There are far more registered Democrats in this country than Republicans. Those of us who are not on the Right must get angry. We must find the issue that will ignite us all. If not because we see the light, then because we feel the heat.

FOCUS ON YOUTH

I have long had the sense that the Right and the Republican party do a far better job of reaching out to young America than we do. I say this because I have a good number of young Republican friends who are constantly approached by the party to get involved. On

the other hand, although I was selected by *Time* magazine as a left of center future leader of America, I have
never been approached by the Democratic party. And
that's part of what's wrong with the Democratic party.

The Right wants you involved because politics is war,
not a spectator sport, and they're trying to line up all
the recruits they can. What better foot soldiers than
young people? (Even though there is nothing in the
Contract with America about making life better for
young Americans.)

Now I don't care that the Democratic party did not
cater to me. My concern is—as a young American with
a history in liberal politics—if *I'm* not being recruited,
how many hundreds of thousands are being ignored as
well?

Bill Clinton campaigned hard for the youth vote in
1992, appearing on MTV and "The Arsenio Hall
Show" to prove he was very concerned about youth
issues. His efforts paid off. He soundly bested George
Bush with the youth vote. Conversely, Clinton protégé
Wyche Fowler of Georgia didn't fare nearly as well in
his reelection campaign to the U.S. Senate in 1992.
When Fowler, in a meeting with young student activists, was asked to support pro-youth issues, he told
them that young people in America didn't vote and
asked why he should "kiss their a_ _." For the remain-
der of the campaign, everywhere Fowler went, young
folks protested. Not surprisingly, Fowler lost the election.

CUT OFF THE FRINGE

Nothing turns off the American electorate like extremism. As I noted earlier, part of the problem people have with American politics today is that so much of it is about ideology. The majority of Americans are far more interested in finding practical, progressive solutions to the problems we face. Extreme ideology (in either direction) turns off the American people. We have to do a better job of disassociating ourselves from the fringe groups that have somehow become identified as the Left.

One of the issues gathering steam across the country is reparations for the enslavement of African Americans in this country. I am opposed to this. How does one calculate the market value for the enslavement of Black people? Reparations is a payoff. I do not want to be paid off. What Black Americans need are not reparations but efforts to refocus on the basic problems that exist in this country: urban decay, the lack of equal employment opportunity and access to education, declining health care, and the increase of guns on our streets. I would much rather have the government spend its money and its time solving the problems that face America: Black and White. I have yet to meet a single African American who is afraid to compete once the playing field is leveled.

While I completely support equal rights for gays and lesbians under the Constitution, there's a movement gaining momentum that's equally distractionary: legalized same-sex marriages. The fact of the matter is that gays and lesbians are still fighting for basic legal protections in housing, employment, and public accommodations. Why in the world are we getting sidetracked by discussions about legalizing gay marriages? Let's deal with the basic facts of fairness first.

When we don't distance ourselves from these kinds of distractions, we play into the hands of the Right and allow them to use these issues and positions as weapons against us.

Protest has its place. If the civil rights movement proved anything, it's that civil disruption works. I believe in peaceful, organized, respectful, and nonviolent disobedience. Many of the tactics and strategies employed by fringe groups only serve as fodder for the Right and end up compromising the Left. Interrupting worship services at St. Patrick's Cathedral, tangling with commuter traffic in major cities, throwing animal blood on individuals who disagree with their cause are all extremist tactics. We can't allow the Right to unfairly label us by the behavior of such groups.

RACE ISN'T EVERYTHING
AND EVERYTHING ISN'T RACE

Race matters. And anyone who tells you otherwise is a visitor from another planet. I certainly am no apologist for racists or discriminatory behavior. Having said that, the quickest way to further anger the conservative "angry White male" population in this country is to unnecessarily and needlessly throw around the word "racist."

It's not that I'm afraid of offending White men—or

anyone else, for that matter. But I know all too well that once we've further antagonized voters on the Right, they will attempt to take their revenge at the ballot box. And so far they've been successful. Unfortunately, those of us on the Left continue to lose too many important elections by the simple margin of our absence at the polls. We either have to put up or shut up.

In California, for example, we are faced in November of 1996 with a ballot proposition called the California Civil Rights Initiative. This measure is intended to repeal affirmative action in public employment, public education, and public contracting throughout the state. I have maintained throughout this debate—and some of my Black colleagues have taken offense to this—that our strategy for fighting this measure should not include calling everyone who supports this misguided policy a racist. The simple truth is that not everyone who opposes affirmative action is against Black Americans or minorities. Dead wrong but not racist. We in the Black community do ourselves a great disservice by labeling all of our opponents with that description.

We have to do a better job of debating sensitive racial issues on their own merits. No matter how often we may be tempted to resort to using race as a hammer to win our point, we must resist when it's genuinely not accurate.

By this I do not mean to suggest that there are not times when a spade must be called a spade. But the ''R'' word must be used only when a policy or individual or organization genuinely *is* racist.

WORDS HAVE MEANING

One of the things about the Right that I admire as a tactic but hate as a distortion is their uncanny ability to use and often abuse certain words and phrases to codify their message and unfairly represent those of us on the Left. They use words as weapons.

The Right routinely will describe someone as "pro-abortion" rather than "pro-choice." They prefer "welfare state" to public assistance. They've managed to make "liberal" a dirty word. The fact is, we don't play the game as well as they do when it comes to framing the debate. One could argue that there's little honor in such name-calling and that doing so detracts from serious debate about the issues. But in this era of the six-second soundbite, it becomes imperative to get our point across as quickly as possible. The way to do that is to realize that words have power, and to use them to strike fast and effectively.

We have to be more creative about how we get that message across. We've got to learn to speak the language of the folks we're talking to.

SOLIDARITY

There's a fundamental question that the Left must ask in trying to communicate what we stand for: Are we attempting to fashion a consensus?

I believe that we have spent too much time trying to get everybody to agree on everything. Clearly, the Right is a far more homogenous group than we are. We have a much larger conference table. There are more voices and more views. That's not a negative and we should make no apologies. It only means that a greater cross-section of America understands and agrees with our basic tenets.

However, we have no less a mandate, no less a responsibility to exit that room with a plan of action around which we've modeled a consensus. Understandably, we may be holed up a little while longer, but we cannot counter the Right in any uniform way without some sense of solidarity. Imagine America's armed forces trying to attack some foreign enemy with each division making its own calls and acting without coordination.

We get criticized often for being a party that has so many different and divergent interests. Sometimes I get the sense that we ourselves buy into the notion that our party is too big and that we speak for too many. Our greatest strength, like America's, is our diversity. Don't let anyone tell you otherwise.

Conversely, our diversity makes it easier for the Right to play one group against another. Abraham Lincoln was right: "A house divided against itself cannot stand."

The Right understands this very clearly and seeks out and exploits certain "wedge" issues in an attempt to divide and conquer us. Only after we've agreed upon our agenda and created a sense of solidarity can we get back to necessary day-to-day efforts to register people to vote, mount phone campaigns, establish walking precincts, and put together all of the other essential activist tools that we must utilize to win elections.

3

Talk Radio

The Conservative Citadel

According to a survey conducted in 1993 by the Times Mirror Center for the People and the Press, America has one thousand talk-radio stations, up from less than two hundred only a decade ago. There are 3,200 radio talk shows, one half of which are devoted to public policy. Here are some sobering facts about talk radio today:

- News/Talk is the second most listened to format on air, after adult-contemporary music.

- One half of all American adults listen to talk radio; one out of six of them listen regularly.
- Nine of ten political talk-radio listeners are registered to vote, compared with an overall average of six out of ten Americans.
- Only 27 percent of talk-radio listeners voted in 1992 for Bill Clinton.

So much for the "liberal media" bias.

Conservative ideologues insist they're fighting a war against the liberal media. I always ask in response: What bias are they talking about? More adults listen to radio than read the newspaper or watch television. And 70 percent of talk-radio hosts publicly identify themselves as conservatives.

Radio is a constant in our lives. It accompanies us to the office and home again in our cars; we wake up to radio in the morning; we play it throughout the day at home; and some of us even play it at work. Radio is everywhere. Because we live in a society where people are constantly on the run, we often don't have time to read the newspaper every day. And by the end of the day, we're so tired, we're dozing through the nightly news to formulate our opinions about the public policy issues that affect our daily lives. And so many rely more heavily on talk radio. What we get, as a result, is conservative propaganda and diatribe, which, because many listeners haven't taken the time to research the issues fully, skews their views and perspective, resulting in their voting conservative.

If anything, there's a conservative bias in much of today's media. Moreover, there's a distinct difference between how the mainstream, so-called "liberal media," such as network news, operates and how conservative talk radio works:

1. THEY LIE

Any news story you see on national or local television or read in print has to be based on the facts, on some semblance of objective truth. That's not the case on talk radio, where hosts are at liberty to say whatever they want, however they want, whenever they want. On talk radio, the truth is what each of us determines it to be. No facts are required, no attribution is necessary. The only thing that matters is pulling in the ratings and advertising dollars. If the numbers are there, talk-radio hosts can state the most outrageous exaggerations as fact, and get away with it.

Here are some examples of talk radio's most notorious conservative host, Rush Limbaugh, who's infamous for stretching the truth into unrecognizable shapes in order to substantiate his extremist views, taken from *EXTRA!,* the bimonthly newsletter of FAIR (Fairness and Accuracy in Reporting).

THE LIE: "The poorest people in America are better off than the mainstream families of Europe."

THE REALITY: The average annual income of the poorest 20 percent of Americans is $5,226; the average income in dollars of European nations—Germany, France, the United Kingdom, and Italy—is $19,708. One has to wonder the last time Rush actually came face-to-face with a poor person. Has he visited some of our nation's pools of poverty? Does he know of what he speaks? *Forbes,* by the way, estimates Limbaugh's own income for the years 1992–1994 at a cool $25 million.

THE LIE: "There are more American Indians alive today than there were when Columbus arrived or at any other time in history. Does this sound like a record of genocide?"

THE REALITY: The U.S. Bureau of Indian Affairs estimates the Native American population before the arrival of Columbus at between 5 million and 15 million in the United States, compared with 2 million today. Millions died as a result of disease, wars, and famine.

THE LIE: "Women were doing quite well in this country before feminism came along."

THE REALITY: It was only in the last seventy-five years that women were given the right to vote. The vast majority were discouraged from attending college or entering a profession until recent decades.

Rush isn't the only ideologue out there, he's just got the biggest mouth. There's a whole cadre of conservative talk-show hosts who behave just as irresponsibly as Rush, spreading half-truths and outright lies to further their agenda and inflame the passions of the uninformed.

2. MONOLOGUE, NOT DIALOGUE

A news story, whether in print or on television or radio, explores both sides of the issue. This is not the case on conservative talk radio.

Most of the liberal shows are guest-driven and debate both sides of the issues of the day. Conservatives who host talk shows aren't interested in debating with those who don't agree with them. They're interested in monologue, not dialogue.

These hosts believe that, given the "liberal media bias," they *are* equal time. Consequently, they could care less about what you or I think when we disagree with the conservative agenda.

3. FREE SPEECH?

There is no such thing as a retraction on a radio talk show. Hosts don't apologize, recant, or otherwise clarify anything they may have said that is derogatory, demeaning, or even racist over the air. These conservative hosts are far more interested in "shock value" than with the time-honored American values of truth, fairness, or even accuracy.

KFI-Los Angeles's Emiliano Lamon once had the gall to suggest on the public airwaves that homeless people "should be put to sleep." In other words, they should be killed. Even after the station received many outraged letters and calls, the top boss at KFI refused to ask Lamon to apologize. The stations' token response was to ask him to "reassess his feelings." When pressed on the issue of allowing a KFI employee to advocate first-degree murder, KFI's manager, Howard Neal, tried to evade the criticism in an interview with *The Los Angeles Times:* "If people are looking to be negative about it, you could make that assumption. I would not, personally, make that assumption."

Joe Crummey of L.A.'s KMPC, where I hosted an evening show, once suggested that O. J. Simpson was guilty and, therefore, listeners should take justice into their own hands by going to the jail and taking Simpson outside to "string him up."

Driving to work one night, I heard another KMPC host, Xavier Hermosillo, tell a Black female caller that the problem with Black people was that they were lazy, are lifetime welfare dependents, and that Black women are so promiscuous that they don't know who the fathers of their babies are.

The next day I wrote a letter to Hermosillo, telling him that his comments were demeaning and racist and that I had lost all respect for him. I also complained to the management of the station about his racist diatribe; although he was called on the carpet by management, he was never forced to apologize.

Examples of this kind of behavior on talk radio are endless.

G. Gordon Liddy, the convicted Watergate felon turned conservative radio talk host, went on the air and openly suggested shooting Alcohol, Tobacco, and Firearms (ATF) agents. In fact, not only did he advocate shooting them, he gave tips on how to do it, instructing his listeners to stay away from the chest.

"They've got a vest on underneath," he said. "Head shots. Head shots."

Liddy was criticized profusely but offered no apology and received no reprimand. Instead, in 1995, he was honored with a freedom of speech award from the National Association of Radio Talk Show Hosts.

But, of course, the talk-radio hosts are only one facet of conservative talk radio. Callers and guests add far more fuel and vitriol to the public "debate." A caller phoned WABC in New York during the 1989 mayoral campaign with a warning that the city would be overrun by "Black welfare parasites" if Black candidate David Dinkins was elected. A Catholic priest told a Colorado Springs audience that God wants gays dead and that Jews and minorities shouldn't mix.

What's especially troubling about all of this is that the Right conducts these on-air "character assassinations" under the guise and protection of the First Amendment, claiming that our country is going to hell and that we have to take it back. They justify this kind of un-American behavior—calling for the quarantining of AIDS victims, or urging American citizens to turn back or even shoot illegal immigrants—by the most sacred of documents, the United States Constitution.

If that isn't an outrage, I don't know what is.

But it's not all bleak. Talk radio has the potential to be a wonderful tool. What I like about talk radio is that it allows, in a very democratic way, the American public to involve and engage themselves in a debate about the most pressing issues of our time. We often don't put forth enough effort to let elected officials and others know how we feel about various issues and events. Talk radio allows for that. It's the barbershop of the 1990s, with a speaker. Participation is free to all. Most calls to talk radio are local or toll-free.

Talk radio also allows for a diversity of thought. On television and in print, you get the news the news agencies feel is important—and much of it deals with the extremes of life—only those elements or events that can be capsulized in an interesting or sensational story. Sure, there are different reporters and anchors, but you still get the same slant, the same perspective, day in and day out. On talk radio, once the host has given you his or her opinions, the show revolves around several hours of callers who say exactly what they think as well.

That's important in large cities like New York and Los Angeles, where often people aren't otherwise involved in the lives of many of those around them. By listening to talk radio, you can become exposed to several very different slices of life without getting out of your car.

Before I started doing talk radio, I did my daily commentary, "The Smiley Report," on smaller Black radio stations that allowed me the same luxury conservative hosts have: to preach to the choir. So I know what it's like to come on the radio every day and say whatever I wanted, with my audience in total agreement with nearly everything I said.

Nonetheless, I was responsible about it. I didn't make racist or demeaning remarks. I didn't incite people to violence.

I am certainly not alone in seeing the negative impact of talk radio. After the Oklahoma City bombing, which put the issue of right-wing extremism on the front pages of every newspaper in the country, President Clinton himself tore into the current state of conservative talk radio, denouncing those who "spread hate" and use "reckless speech and behavior" on radio airwaves. "People are encouraging conduct that will undermine the fabric of this country," said Clinton. "If you preach hate," said Clinton earlier, "you get a talk show. If you preach love, you get a yawn."

I couldn't agree more.

Talk radio doesn't have to be a threat to the sort of reasoned and rational debate Americans need on the issues of the day. But as long as we have talk-show hosts who are irresponsible in their use of their powerful and popular medium, the threat is real.

On WABC in New York, ultra-right-winger Bob Grant referred to former Mayor David Dinkins as "the men's room attendant" and described National Organization for Women president Patricia Ireland as "that ugly dyke." He hangs up on callers who disagree with him, yelling, "Go clean my toilet!" or "I don't need my shoes shined."

On Atlanta's WSB radio, in a city that's predominately Black, conservative talk-radio host Neal Boortz described a recent arrest of three boys for robbery at their mother's home this way: "When police came to her welfare house and knocked on this welfare queen's door and took her little predators away, this woman, who by the way was about the size of a phone booth—she obviously puts her food stamps and welfare checks to good use—she was screaming like a stuck pig because the police were taking her little predator welfare tickets away!"

Need I say more?

One of my biggest complaints with talk radio is that it doesn't provide an equal opportunity for women and persons of color. Very few serve as on-air personalities. Although the popularity of talk radio continues to rise, the opportunities for all who are not conservative White males have not grown accordingly. A 1994 survey could only come up with 14 Black talk-radio hosts and just one Latino host of a national radio show. In a medium of over 3,000 talk-radio programs, this survey found only 138 female hosts, and a mere 57 of them were hosting issue-oriented programs.

Shameful.

The station managers would have you believe that women and Black listeners have no interest in talk radio. Not true.

Let me tell you about my personal experience. When I joined KABC's morning show, the "Ken and Barkley Company," it ranked number nine with Black listeners. But after I'd been there for a little while as the only Black commentator on L.A. mainstream radio, the show went from ninth to third place with Black listeners. As I often say, it's not as if I speak for the entire Black community. Black folks don't meet at my house for dinner every Sunday after church to formulate our opinions. It's just that for the first time African American listeners were hearing from someone who shared their experiences. And they spread the word.

Later, as part of the first African American/Latino Generation X radio talk team in the country on KABC's sister station KMPC, we attracted a significant number of Black and Latino phone callers every single night, in addition to our sizable White audience. These folks had never called in to a talk-radio show before because there wasn't one that talked about their issues.

Every Tuesday night, during the second hour of our show, we had a segment called "On the Move," featuring outstanding young Americans who were serving their community and their country. As a result, we attracted an enormous and energized youthful audience as well. We offered a different viewpoint and listeners responded. The truth is that if more women, people of color, liberals, and young Americans are given the opportunity to participate in talk radio, more of them will listen and join in the debate. It's that simple.

One of the things I respect about President Clinton is that he kept his pledge to make his Cabinet look like America. His Cabinet is the most ethnically and culturally diverse in the history of this country. And in a participatory democracy, that's the way things ought to be. Right, Rush?

Same goes for talk radio. It needs to sound more like America looks.

Some argue that talk radio has no impact on public opinion or public policy. Georgetown University professor Diane Owen told *USA Today* that talk-radio hosts have been "really ineffective in getting any kind of community action stirred up. There's a big difference between creating attitudes and creating an environment of alienation and displeasure and instigating people to take action . . . it's a lot of talk and no action."

Yet, the seventy-three Republican freshmen who came to Congress following the November 1994 elections attributed their stunning victory to Rush

Limbaugh and other conservative talk-radio hosts, citing polls that showed people who listen to talk radio ten hours or more per week voted Republican three-to-one.

Clearly, talk radio *is* effective. The Right has been using the medium to try to "take back America," by pushing a platform that is pro-life, pro-gun, pro-business, pro-tobacco, pro-school prayer, anti-affirmative action, anti-immigration, anti-individual rights, anti-women, and anti-gays.

Again, not dialogue. Monologue.

Up to now, the Right has very effectively made talk radio their own.

"When the switch of music to FM radio opened up the AM band to talk radio in the 1980s, it was conservatives who had the vitality and the desire to flock to a new medium and create their own culture there," *Reason* magazine editor Virginia Postrel told *The New York Times* in 1995.

"Talk radio is right-wing for the same reason that free weekly newspapers are left-wing," she said. "They're both examples of how a newly abundant medium comes to be dominated by a group with intellectual vitality that is outside the political mainstream."

As the conservative talk-show phenomenon started to gather steam, programmers added more and more of them. The copycat syndrome kicked in. And why not? Most of the station managers are conservatives who like what their boys are saying.

Talk radio is the most segregated format in radio. This is partly because 90 percent of the top managers in talk radio, not unlike print and television, are White men. Black listeners, other persons of color, and those on the Left don't generally feel welcome in the talk-radio genre, so they turn to other programming or media. Frankly, talk radio is far more segregated than society at large.

For African Americans in a few select cities, there are a handful of Black talk stations. The reason these stations exist in the first place is because mainstream stations don't hire Black commentators. The irony is that these conservative programmers and talk-show hosts are the ones who preach about living in a color-blind society. But they say one thing and do another. As a result, Black Americans call their stations, White conservatives phone their stations, White liberals have virtually no one to call, and nobody's talking to one another. (An additional reason talk radio stays so segregated, apart from conservative bias, of course, is because of the sponsors. Play me a commercial cluster, and I'll tell you the makeup of the audience. Apparently, many advertisers are not interested in expanding their audience. In any major city, the group most undervalued and least sought after by talk radio stations are persons of color.)

I believe the programmers just aren't interested in adding a little intellectual or racial color to the traditional talk-radio audience. They tailor their shows to their market. I suppose that's natural. A station that plays country and western caters to a country audience. A station that plays Top 40 plays to an audience that loves the hits. They play to their audience like talk radio does to its audience. The difference is that talk radio has an impact on the direction of this country.

Unlike a station that plays Travis Tritt and Garth Brooks or Janet Jackson and Snoop Doggy Dogg, these stations spend their days and evenings talking about public policy. They have a responsibility to make the stations sound more like America as a whole.

One of the more disturbing trends to me in the last few years has been the rise of the Black conservative talk-radio host. I'm thinking of radio hosts such as Ken Hamblin of Denver and Armstrong Williams of Washington, D.C., who have found a niche by saying all the rabid, reactionary things the extreme Right wants to hear.

Ken Hamblin, for example, calls Denver's Black neighborhoods "dark town," and the people who live there "dark people." He repeatedly refers to Black political leaders as "spooks" and once retorted that free speech "is something dark little people like you [the National Black Caucus] could never understand." He denigrates Black leaders, saying, "Show me one—just one—city that has prospered under Black leadership." He routinely hands out "absolution from White guilt" certificates. Of affirmative action, he has wryly said, "You can't save all the crybabies" and declares that he doesn't want to hear "any more Black folks lying in the dying cockroach position, whining."

Hamblin's outrageous rhetoric might be funny if his vile and repugnant diatribe wasn't taken so seriously by the Right. My initial reaction was to just ignore him. But one night on the radio, when I was discussing Nation of Islam leader Louis Farrakhan's latest barrage of anti-Semitic remarks, suggesting that we only encouraged him to make inflammatory statements by giving him national exposure, a Jewish listener called in, arguing that you can't ignore people who make these kinds of disgusting statements. If nobody challenges them, and we let this kind of behavior slide, it is certain to continue, and perhaps even escalate. And I realized he was right. That caller taught me a very important lesson. I'd love to ignore Ken Hamblin, but what he says on radio and television simply cannot be laughed off.

Armstrong Williams isn't as incendiary as Hamblin. But he is in the Right place at the Right time with the Right message—indeed, his radio program is called "The Right Side."

Following the November 1994 elections, Williams said, "Conservatives in the Black community hold the keys to the kingdom. In abandoning the liberal faith, we stand only to lose a ruling philosophy that has brought us nowhere since the 1960s. Despite billions of federal dollars poured into welfare programs and pork brought to the cities by liberal Democrats, the condition of Blacks has not improved. The Republican party is the natural home for the vast majority of Blacks interested in safe streets, economic prosperity, faith, family, and personal responsibility. Now more than ever, we need to break away from the crippling political orthodoxy that has kept us begging for crumbs at the back stoop of the Democratic plantation."

It's true that Black Americans have not been given the respect they deserve from the Democratic party, given their loyalty through the years. But Williams is out of his mind to suggest that Black conservatives "hold the keys to the kingdom." Maybe the latrine, but that's about it. Never has the party of Strom Thurmond (whom Williams calls his mentor) or Jesse Helms done anything—certainly not willingly—to help the plight of Black people in this country. The party of Kennedy and Johnson has. I shudder to think where Black America would be today, had it not been for the Civil Rights Act or the Voting Rights Act, ideas it took quite a long while for the other party to warm up to.

Furthermore, it is downright foolhardy to suggest that Black Americans are becoming more conservative in the 1990s. If anything, African Americans, tired of being taken for granted, are becoming more radical or apathetic.

So Black conservatives—all ten of them—might just as well stay in the closet, because that's exactly where they belong.

Hamblin, calling himself "the Black Avenger," boasts that he can say things "that a White person couldn't get away with." Which is precisely the problem with Black conservatives on mainstream talk radio. They pontificate and offer positions that are antithetical to the best interests of Black America and society at large. And they can get away with it, simply because they are Black, and White liberals dare not take them on. They do nothing more than provide cover and justification for White male conservatives who can't get away with uttering such racist and discriminatory comments.

The reason these talk shows have caught on is because White bigots who share these outlandish views can now justify their positions and even persuade themselves that Black people, at least candid, "smart" Black people, feel the same way they do. And if Black

Americans feel likewise, White conservatives don't have to feel guilty or apologetic about what they believe.

So, when these hosts go on the air and preach their anti-Black message, they provide the ammunition to listeners who want to point a finger at Black America for everything that's wrong with this country.

And from the point of view of Hamblin and Williams, such controversy adds to media coverage, which equals ratings. And that's what they care about. Most Blacks are repulsed by these claims and when they are able to get through on the air, let Hamblin and Williams have it.

Every programmer in the country now seems to want a Black conservative host. The station gets a lot for their money—a conservative, controversy, and someone who's Black to blunt criticism from the community about their ineffectual minority hiring practices.

When KABC, my home station, was attempting to fill a slot in their prime-time lineup, they reportedly went looking specifically for a Black conservative. It's the feel-good hire of the 1990s. Ken Hamblin from KNUS in Denver turned the job down, reportedly because he didn't want to do talk radio in such a "liberal" city. Eventually, they hired a Black conservative from Cleveland.

The point is, whether the radio talk-show host is a White conservative or a Black conservative, the Right has dominated the fight for the airwaves. It's now time to do something about it before it's too late.

For starters, it bothers me when people casually say that they listen to Rush Limbaugh or some other right-wing ideologue because they find them entertaining, or they want to hear what they have to say. We *know* what they're saying. They spew the same tired drumbeat of negativity, hate, and "Take back America" cant day in and day out. Is that entertaining? Remember, whoever makes up part of the listening audience contributes to the shows' ratings, thus helping to keep them on the air.

Stop listening!

Second, when we do hear the kind of claptrap rhetoric that gets us so frustrated and angry that we just about want to jump into the radio itself to ring their necks, we should call the show and express our opposition to their innuendo and propaganda. If ever we are going to turn the tide against this kind of hate and irresponsible tirade, we have to at least make our own voices and positions heard.

As I mentioned earlier, one of the things I like about the Right is their organizational smarts (i.e., letter-writing and phone-in campaigns). We need to employ these same organizational skills to fight talk-radio ranting. Getting a talk show off the air simply because the public disagrees with its philosophy or political persuasion is not easy. In fact, it's darn near impossible. However, a constant and increasing barrage of telephone calls and letters does have an impact on the way management views a show or a specific talk-show host. Let's swing the tide of public response against such hate-mongering. After all, it all comes down to ratings. And if enough people speak up and out, perhaps we can silence the Right's talk-show tirades and restore to the airwaves a reservoir of reason.

4

The Big Tent

There are certain individuals on the Right that I have admiration for. Empower America codirector Jack Kemp is one of them.

I think Kemp did a respectable job as Housing Secretary and I was somewhat saddened when he decided to not enter the race for the 1996 GOP presidential nomination, because of all the potential Republican contenders, Kemp was the only one who seemed to care about expanding the base of the Republican party. Kemp talked early and often about making the GOP a "big tent" party.

Ultimately, Kemp decided not to seek the White House, citing the excessive amount of money he'd have to raise to become a significant player. But I also believe Kemp realized that the message of inclusion and tolerance that he was preaching was falling on deaf ears. It wasn't a message conservatives wanted to hear, particularly with the religious Right dominating the party platform.

Kemp came to realize what we've known all along. The Right represents little more than a small tepee of the privileged, the lucky, and the well connected. It is those of us on the Left who have always represented the best interests of all Americans.

Like far too many American families, certainly Black ones, no one in my immediate family had ever participated in the political process. So when it came time for me to register to vote, there was no family tradition or guiding political philosophy that led me to the Left. If anything, growing up in Indiana, I should have registered as a Republican.

But I knew that Ronald Reagan didn't care about me or anyone else who wasn't born with a silver spoon in his or her mouth. As well liked as Reagan was as a man, he had no knowledge of or interest in all those Americans of varying backgrounds, hues, and beliefs who didn't grow up or live like him. I like to believe that every American is entitled to a quality education, a decent job, and security in old age; that one's talent and attitude should be the sole determinants of one's altitude.

I'd like to say that I was drawn to the "big tent" of the Left by divine intervention. But I don't want to mix politics and religion. There's enough of that going on already. More accurately, I was drawn to the Left because ours is a group that shows concern and compassion, one that believes in inclusion and abhors intolerance.

As I noted earlier, I think most Americans prefer political solutions that are practical rather than strictly ideological, which are often restricting.

The Right is concerned more with ideology than good ideas. They prefer the politics of negativism, of repeal and rescind, of prescribe and prohibit, rather than investigating new ideas that will take us forward. I guess new ideas hurt some minds like new shoes hurt some feet.

You see, I'm firmly convinced that most Americans believe in the fundamental *fairness* espoused by the Left, not the *favoritism* of the Right. Consequently, our job is to fashion a consensus and a plan of action around an agenda that doesn't play favorites but is fundamentally fair to all Americans. An agenda that is practical in its approach to problem-solving and moves the nation ahead. One that is progressive rather than regressive.

In Chapter 2 of this book, I suggested that we must articulate not just what we are against, but what we are for. What does it mean to be on the Left? What common beliefs do we hold that set us apart from the Right?

In the church I attend, as part of our Sunday morning worship service, we regularly share with visitors and friends a short, scripted presentation on what "we believe." For the members, it is always a very moving part of the program because it reminds us why we are there. First-time visitors appreciate the presentation because it succinctly and clearly explains our purpose, our core values, and our beliefs.

I think there are a number of ideals that distinguish the Left, and which transcend the politics of individual groups or factions. Below, I list the twelve core beliefs that I think define the Left and help to shape our specific goals and ideals.

WE BELIEVE

In Individual Rights

What's most frightening about the Right? Their attempt to legislate morality and trample on the constitutional rights and freedoms of individuals. We believe in the right to free expression. The right to not be discriminated against. The right to not be pressured to pray in school, or at any governmentally mandated time or place not of our own choosing. The right to reproductive choice. Civil rights. The right to life, liberty, and the pursuit of happiness.

The Right invariably wants to abridge our personal freedoms. Americans of every race, political persuasion, and religion must rebuff the efforts of the Right to inflict their beliefs on us and infringe upon our constitutional liberties.

America has real problems that demand real solutions. A rollback of our rights can only exacerbate the problems we already face. Poverty, crime, the deterioration of our infrastructure, and the inequality of our educational system will not be magically cured by restricting personal freedoms.

Most of us have worked too hard, sacrificed too much, and waited too long to give up our inalienable and God-given rights. Can we afford to sit back now and let the Right chip away at those hard-won freedoms?

If such rights are worth fighting to get, then they are certainly worth fighting to keep.

In Safe Neighborhoods and Streets

Each election the Republicans trot out the motto "Get tough on crime." It's a reliable campaign slogan. But crime is not a Republican issue—it is an issue that concerns all Americans. Most of us rank crime as one of our greatest concerns. We all know someone who has been victimized—if we have not been victimized ourselves. We all want safe streets and the right to live our lives without fear.

So far, the Right has pushed only two politically expedient ideas to combat crime—tougher sentences, including truth-in-sentencing laws, and making prison time as harsh as possible for convicts. Once again, their ideas are only half-right.

Although we must not be afraid or unwilling to stiffen sentences for the most violent offenders, and require that most violent felons serve at least 85 percent of their prison term, any comprehensive crime control strategy must include prevention education, treatment, and rehabilitation as well.

While we haggle with the Right about punishment

versus prevention, our nation's most violent repeat offenders are being let loose on the streets again.
Tougher sentences and crime prevention are not mutually exclusive. In fact, our impassioned argument for
greater prevention is significantly enhanced when we
show that we are unafraid to make those who commit
the crime serve their time.

Specific proposals for how to lower crime vary—as
do proposals from the Right. Personally, I support
tougher sentences and truth in sentencing for the
most violent felons. I would also do away with mandatory minimum sentences for drug offenders, not because it's not an attractive idea but because it doesn't
work. It is mandatory sentencing that is primarily responsible for prison overcrowding, causing more violent criminals to be released early. Judiciary discretion
allows jurists to be tough on those who sell drugs and
impose treatment and rehabilitation for drug users.
Drug abuse is first and foremost a health problem, and
secondarily a criminal act. Which is why I was disap-
pointed when President Clinton announced in his
1996 State of the Union Address that he was ap-
pointing a retired military general as the nation's new
drug czar. I felt it again sent the wrong signal. Last, I
feel this notion of getting tough on criminals once
they're locked up is nonsense. No hot meals. Chain
gangs. No television or radio. No conjugal visits. No
recreational activities. No compassionate leave to attend a funeral. No Christmas visits. No Pell education
grants for prisoners. What are we trying to do here,
increase prison violence and help make criminals

worse human beings upon release from prison than they were upon entering?

Although some on the Left are opposed to the death penalty, as I am, many of us are not. On the other hand, I am in favor of a "one strike" mandatory sentence for rape, murder, and child molestation. But one thing is certain for all of us on the Left: Without crime control, we have no control.

In a Government of the People

We believe in a government of and by the people. Not one controlled by big business and special-interest-group PAC funds. But in order to accomplish that, we have to clean up the system and lower the cost of getting elected.

The overwhelming majority of Americans want the system cleaned up. And even though every politician I've ever come in contact with claims to be in favor of it, nothing ever happens. Why?

Everyone agrees that when it comes to reinventing our system, priority number one is getting the money out of politics. But some believe that real money reform is virtually impossible. It isn't. It just takes a handful of courageous and committed elected officials, with the support of "We the People" to start cleaning up the mess. We must push both parties to consider ways to set campaign spending limits. Reduce the cost of television time. Ban corporate campaign contributions. Abolish special-interest subsidies and political action committee (PAC) donations.

As long as money is the mother's milk of politics, the

only change in Washington is the change that jingles in politicians' pockets.

In Good Jobs for All

I think we all agree the country needs more full-time, permanent, high-paying jobs with growth potential. We have too many part-time, temporary, minimum wage, dead-end jobs.

My generation faces the biggest job shortage since the Great Depression of the 1930s. Over half of all workers under the age of twenty-five are paid hourly wages, with annual earnings below the poverty line. Minimum wage has 26 percent less purchasing power today than it did in 1970. And the largest private employer in the United States today is not General Motors but Manpower, Inc.—a temporary employment agency. Indeed, the Bureau of Labor Statistics projects that the number of new college graduates will outpace the number of new jobs by half a million a year, every year, for the rest of the decade. These days, going to college doesn't guarantee you a job, it only gives you four years to worry about getting one.

Unfortunately, these are just the numbers on my generation. There are so many others—particularly wage earners in their forties and fifties—who have lost their jobs to corporate mergers, technology, job exportation, privatization, downsizing, and the general externalization of jobs. These Americans are finding it almost impossible to find comparable jobs again at comparable pay—or, indeed, any job at all.

This kind of lingering unemployment must be addressed by our elected officials. We must make education, job training, research and development, and infrastructure investment part of our national goals. After all, no investment equals no return.

At the same time, we must cut spending and create better jobs to help stimulate economic growth. I think we should start by cutting wasteful programs and eliminating some $85 billion in corporate welfare, which according to the Cato Institute, made up roughly half the deficit in fiscal 1995 alone.

In Lifting the Least Among Us

The "Greed is good" decade of the 1980s is eclipsed only by the harshness of the 1990s.

I am dumbfounded by the Right's efforts to snatch away the social safety net, further punishing the poor just for being poor. Penalizing children born into disadvantaged families; stripping away the fragile supports of those who, through no fault of their own, have lost their jobs and fallen on hard times.

The Right seems to think that financial success is an indicator of moral virtue, that "the survival of the fittest" is a reasonable premise by which to organize a government and steer a society.

We know better. We as a society have an obligation to help the least among us, to provide services and opportunities for all. The Right has always been most interested in rewarding the wealthy and elite. It is the Left that has embraced the populism of the past, and genuinely reached out to the broad middle class and the under-represented poor. Our efforts and our goals should be directed toward all Americans, not just the favored few who control an inordinate percentage of our resources and wealth.

In a Quality Education for Everyone

Our economy requires an ever-higher level of technical ability and math and science skills for the labor market. Yet fewer and fewer young Americans are being academically prepared.

We believe in giving all Americans the kind of quality education that will prepare them for tomorrow. There is a direct correlation between the amount of education our citizens have and the amount of money they earn in professional life. Increasingly, we have become a nation of the well-to-do well-educated—those attending private schools and elite colleges—and those who are not.

There is no better investment of our money than in quality education. For every dollar of federal assistance, the U.S. government earns an average of $4.50 in future tax receipts. Rather than cutting college assistance programs, Head Start, and other school programs, we need to find ways to bring more of our nation's young into the classroom, so that they can help later to build the America of tomorrow.

In Building a Strong Infrastructure

The condition of our nation's infrastructure determines our quality of life. I'm talking about roads, bridges, housing stock, schools, libraries, employment centers. About public transit. About our parks and recreational facilities. Our public buildings. Our water supply. About waste water treatment and waste disposal systems. Our infrastructure to a large measure makes our society possible. It is the physical foundation upon which America is built. For all the criticism from the Right leveled at FDR's New Deal, it was FDR's Works Progress Administration (WPA) that employed some 8 million people from 1935 to 1941 and built much of our physical infrastructure.

For the last two decades, we have neglected the maintenance and upgrading of that infrastructure. The social, environmental, and health risks now posed are daunting. Without strong bridges, tunnels, and roads, we cannot get to work. Without clean water, we cannot guarantee our children's health. The fact is, repairing and rebuilding our physical infrastructure will help create jobs and spark economic growth. Nowhere is unemployment higher than in our nation's large urban areas, and that's precisely where many infrastructure improvements are most needed. Putting people to work maintaining and improving our public infrastructure is good for both the community and the country in general.

But this reality hasn't convinced cities, states, and the federal government to do much about the decay of our infrastructure. The estimated cost, in 1989 dollars, of rebuilding the nation's highways and bridges alone was $40 billion per year, beginning in 1989 and lasting through the end of the century. I'm afraid to tell you how little we've actually spent annually on infrastructure investment since that report, even though fewer and fewer of our public works are being rated adequate. The steady decline in the quantity and quality of our public infrastructure is scary.

The infrastructure is part of the glue that binds our society together. It is public investment for public good—and not something to be deleted simply because it doesn't benefit corporate bottom lines or the lifestyles of the wealthy.

In Protecting Our Health and Our Future

As citizens of the richest nation on Earth, we believe that every American deserves a basic level of health care—and a health system that can successfully bring that about. We also believe that our elderly retired workers over the age of sixty-five deserve a minimum level of income in return for years of being responsible workers and taxpayers.

There's a very simple reason why American health care has not been reformed and Social Security has not been reinvented, despite the fact that most voters place health care reform as a high priority, and the Social Security system may no longer exist by the time many are ready to retire. The powerful Washington lobbyists know all too well that health care reform and Social Security solvency are inextricably linked together. The solvency of the latter directly depends on the reform of the former. We're talking about the two most powerful special interests in Washington, the health care industry and the senior citizens' American Association of Retired Persons (AARP). It's no wonder that practically any and every recommendation hits resistance.

In polls taken since the GOP gained control of Congress in 1994, Americans continue to express strong support for modest changes in the health care system, as opposed to major reform. President Clinton's call for a major overhaul of the system may have been something of an overreach. But with an estimated 38 million Americans without health care coverage, most of whom are women and children, Americans do want to start somewhere. According to one survey, if health insurance cannot be provided to all Americans, voters favor covering children first, followed by working people who are uninsured.

Given the growing cynicism of many Americans about government, it's really no surprise that many people are afraid of a burdensome government bureaucracy in a reformed health care system. But we must insist on at least starting to cover certain groups who do not have health insurance, and slowly but steadily working toward comprehensive universal health care for all Americans.

At the same time, we must firmly but fairly insist that Social Security be reinvented in the best interests of all Americans. As 46 million Baby Boomers enter retirement beginning in the year 2012, we may find ourselves in the midst of a generational warfare if we don't reform Social Security now. If we wait to deal with it when Social Security is in crisis mode, there will only be two choices, and neither is pretty: a sudden and dramatic increase in taxes, or an ungodly slashing of benefits to senior citizens. Neither option is acceptable. And both are avoidable if we start now.

Social Security is the largest single expenditure of

the federal government, and at current levels, spending on Social Security will have increased by 36 percent at the turn of the century. We give $30 billion annually in benefits to retirees earning an after-tax income of more than $100,000; half of those retirees are millionaires. The average senior citizen has paid just under $84,000 into Social Security, and yet will get back more than $300,000.

In 1994, the Bipartisan Commission on Entitlement and Tax Reform warned that Social Security could go into deficit as early as 2013, primarily because the ratio of workers to retirees is shrinking. In 1950, there were sixteen workers to every retiree. Today there are but five workers to every retiree. By the year 2030, there will be less than three. It's projected that Social Security will run up a long-range deficit of $59 billion annually over the next seventy-five years.

Sadly, both the Right and the Left play partisan politics on this matter. We believe Social Security is a fundamental government program—and one that must be saved. What was meant to provide a security blanket for elderly workers with few financial resources must not be drained by those who are well enough off to not need those vital funds. It is not meant to be a federal savings account. It was the Left that created Social Security, and we must now chart a course toward solvency and security.

In Protecting the Environment

Apparently, being a conservative has nothing to do with "conserving" or "conservation."

The Right would have us believe that acid rain, dumping toxic wastes, contaminating our groundwater, using up our nonrenewable resources, cutting down old-growth forest, and exterminating various species do not have an injurious effect on our environment. In fact, they have done everything possible to relax if not repeal environmental protection laws. Every year hundreds of millions of our tax dollars go to subsidize companies that degrade the environment, as well as to pay for cleaning up their toxic messes. Future generations will continue to pay, not just with their wallets but with their health and quality of life.

We believe in preserving our natural heritage for our children—while balancing the very real needs of business and the nation today. Unwittingly or otherwise, however, the Left has contributed to the general public's lack of awareness and interest in protecting our planet. In spite of my respect for their efforts to preserve our resources, I have three major criticisms of the environmental movement.

First, the environmental movement is primarily a movement run by well-to-do White liberals. Organizers have not done enough to expand the core of the environmental leadership to include and involve representatives of communities of color and people of varying social classes. As a result, a great many people feel alienated from the movement—not the smartest way to galvanize the country around an issue.

Second, although by now most of us have heard the words "Reduce, reuse, and recycle," this message isn't clearly understood in poor and minority communities. We need more education on preserving and restoring our environment targeted at all peoples, not just a narrow segment of the American population.

Finally, while environmental activists are long on seeing the environmental threats and problems, they come up short on grappling with the economic concerns of the specific regions and communities involved. Put frankly, most who live and work in indigenous communities are worried, first and foremost, about their jobs, their families, and their homes before they can grapple with the larger environmental concerns of clean air, fresh water, and the ecology.

If we really care about protecting our planet, we have to do a better job of linking the threats to our environment to the harsh realities of our economy. Reasonable compromise is a virtue, not a failing. We may have to sacrifice a stand on old-growth forests at times to appropriately respond to job concerns or the real need for utilizing natural resources. On the other hand, we cannot allow industry practices that will permanently pollute and destroy our land, air, and water.

In Fiscal Responsibility

As much as I hate the phrase "tax and spend" as a label describing the Left's fiscal policies, it is a term that has stuck like an annoying gummy sticker. The truth is that "tax and spend" best describes how Washington at large works. It's not a question of Right or Left, Republican or Democrat. The Left may have been more inclined to raise taxes to fund new programs in the past, but that is no longer true. We understand and agree that we as a nation must be fiscally responsible,

and that entitlement funding—and funding for all social programs—must be paid for by tax cuts in other
areas.

To a great extent, balancing the budget, deficit reduction, and paying down the debt are all linked to
one important factor that Washington politicians avoid
like the plague: reeling in the runaway costs of entitlement spending. We were warned by a bipartisan panel
in 1994 that if left unchecked, entitlements will grow to
account for nearly 60 percent of all federal spending
by 2003, and that by 2030 they will consume all antici-
pated federal revenues.

How does that compare with previous decades?
Spending for mandatory federal programs and the interest on debt accounted for only thirty cents of every
federal dollar collected and spent in 1963. By the year
2003, they will account for seventy-two cents of every
dollar. Social Security, Medicare, Medicaid, and civil
service pensions will account for three-fourths of those
expenditures. The main reason for the growth in entitlement spending is the soaring cost of health care.

I could cover the remaining pages of this book with
numbers about the coming apocalypse, but I think you
get the picture; either we cut entitlements or raise
taxes.

There are many ways to accomplish this: raising the
eligibility age for Social Security, means-testing for certain programs, curbing tax entitlements such as tax deductions for mortgage interest or employers' contributions for medical insurance, changing investment
strategies for the trust funds that finance various entitlements, or a combination of the above.

But we cannot escape the problems of tomorrow by ignoring them today.

In a Moral Awakening

It might surprise you to know that when asked what troubled them most, 62 percent of Christian Coalition members cited a sense of "general moral decline." Only 10 percent cited abortion.

They are right. Undeniably, we have experienced a moral decay in America. We need only open our eyes and unplug our ears. But since when has respect for responsibility, for decency, and for a humane society been a conservative quality? We on the Left believe just as strongly in family, in God and religion, in right and wrong, in justice and generosity, kindness, courage, and commitment to our communities. It is the Left that advocates reining in violent crime by registering guns, that opposes the tidal wave of violence on television and in the media. Yes, we believe in tolerance and freedom of choice—but we also believe in helping our brothers and sisters, our fellow men.

Generally speaking, the moral concerns of the Right are rooted in a kind of negativism: Thou shalt not. As always, the devil is in the details. The way the Right would like to go about slowing or reversing the moral decline in America is by banning free speech, free choice, and all behavior and lifestyles that aren't the same as their own.

For example, what was accomplished by Empower America codirector William J. Bennett and C. Delores Tucker, chairwoman of the National Political Congress of Black Women, when they pressured Time Warner about its marketing of rap music? To be sure, we can do without some rap music, particularly what's known as "gangsta rap." Indeed, many Black radio stations refuse to play rap. Yet, rap music generally is no less viable an art form than rock music. In the end, a legitimate form of free expression had been vilified, rap artists had not been involved in the conversation and subsequently not challenged to do better, and when all was said and done, Time Warner unloaded the successful Interscope Records, but the music of Snoop Doggy Dogg and Dr. Dre plays on.

The same is true with the attack on daytime television talk shows by Bennett and Democratic senators Joseph I. Lieberman and Sam Nunn. Without question, the daytime television talkfests would benefit from a strong dose of civility. As an African American, I believe that daytime talk is the worst public exploitation of Black people since slavery.

Dwight Eisenhower once said, "You do not lead by hitting people over the head—that's assault, not leadership." Threatening corporations and clinics, producers and performers, artists and advertisers only hardens people's hearts. We're not reshaping society from the ground up, but only beating a certain segment over the head.

Clearly, a moral crisis exists. Our answer, though, must not be mere condemnation or censorship but a call for responsibility by and for all. I feel our country would benefit from a values education curriculum taught in grade school and high school. Most parents want help in teaching their children a basic sense of right and wrong. Don't accept the claptrap from the Right claiming that only *they* believe in Christian morality. It's just not true.

In Equal Opportunity for All

Sometimes I wonder what kind of America this would be if over the last fifty years we had made as much progress in advancing the causes of our people as we have made in developing "things."

We believe in equal opportunity for all. The Right does not. We push and they pull. We believe in equal rights for women, for people of all colors and ethnic backgrounds. In the rights of children. In civil rights. In voting rights. In no discrimination based on sexual orientation. The only "right" conservatives support is "state's rights." What, may I ask, are so sacred about state's rights? Were the rights that were protected in Mississippi and Alabama in the 1950s a model for the country?

Although America has not always endorsed liberal "policies," the country has and still does embrace the liberal "values" of inclusion, justice, and equal opportunity. A *New York Times*/CBS poll revealed that two-thirds of the public believes that the government should take care of people who cannot care for themselves. Fundamentally, we are still a nation that believes in fairness, not favoritism; in charity, not selfishness.

The Right, however, continues to overplay its hand in supporting policies that propagate inequality. They feel they can justifiably force their ultraconservative values on the rest of us, simply because they are "right." But they are making a huge mistake if they feel they have been given a "mandate" to recreate America.

It has been said that the arc of a moral universe is long, but it bends toward justice. I agree with that. I further believe that what's allowed the Left to make such monumental and lasting contributions to the nation is our moral authority, from which follows the belief that it is dead wrong to discriminate against or deny any human being the right to let his or her talents take that person as far as he or she can go on personal merit. It is wrong. And no value strikes me as more Christian, or more moral, than that.

We believe that reasonable people can agree to disagree on certain matters of consequence. Indeed, some of the very beliefs I list are perhaps worthy of dialogue and debate among ourselves and with the Right. We must continue to hone our vision, to refine our beliefs and define our message. Unlike what many conservatives seem to say, it ain't right just because I said so. But there are two items that I believe are absolutely nonnegotiable for the Left, because they go to the very essence of our being, our purpose, and our individual will.

For me, being on the Left begins and ends with protecting individual rights and guaranteeing an equal opportunity for all—always.

5

Blacklash

The Truth on Affirmative Action

Current conservative ideology has been refueling racial fears by making affirmative action the most divisive issue in America since slavery.

Starting in the late 1940s, the federal government began promoting workplace equality with a series of measures prohibiting discrimination in federal employment. Twenty years later, the Civil Rights Act of 1964 was enacted to prohibit employment discrimination based on sex, race, national origin, or religion. The following year, President Lyndon Johnson signed an executive order establishing the first affirmative action, requiring federal contractors to undertake affirmative action to increase the number of minorities they employed.

It was Republican President Richard Nixon who, in 1969, after Department of Labor hearings uncovered widespread race discrimination in the construction industry, developed the concept of using "goals and timetables" to measure the progress federal construction companies were making in increasing the numbers of Black Americans on their payrolls. A year later, President Nixon extended the use of goals and timetables to all federal contractors, and four years later, declared that such affirmative action programs should also include women, who were historically under-represented.

Affirmative action was established to balance unequal scales. It is a fundamentally fair and necessary remedy for the still-lingering effects of historic injustice, which ultimately benefits all Americans by allowing for the hiring or promoting of all qualified candidates.

In their attempt to overturn hard-won civil rights gains, the Right has distorted the facts about affirmative action, not the least of which is constantly referring to Nixon's flexible concept of "goals and timetables" as rigid "quotas" used to mandate outcomes. They say affirmative action is inherently unfair. Let me deal with the "fairness" issue head-on.

When affirmative action is used improperly, it is without question unfair. Not to mention that it serves as ammunition for the critics. It is wrong when White-owned companies use African Americans as fronts to win minority "set-aside" contracts. When employers deliberately hire unqualified persons or refuse to hire a White male for some unrelated reason, and then insist that affirmative action made them do it, they abuse affirmative action. Whenever employers treat a flexible goal as a quota, or favor the unjustified preference of the unqualified over the qualified—of any race or gender—they misdefine "affirmative action."

Any and all abuses of affirmative action must be investigated fully and brought to an immediate end. But such abuses are not affirmative action, not legal, and not acceptable. They are no reason to abolish this corrective program. Not unless what you're really fighting is economic redistribution.

REVERSE DISCRIMINATION

In 1973, Allan Bakke, a White premed student, applied for enrollment at the University of California–Davis but was denied entrance because of a special admissions program that reserved a specific number of seats (sixteen of one hundred) for qualified minorities. Bakke later discovered that there were minority students who had been admitted with lower grades and test scores than he.

So Bakke sued UC and won, and the country saw the creation of a new concept, commonly referred to as "reverse discrimination." The case went to the Supreme Court in 1978, which struck down the idea of numerical quotas but reconfirmed the notion of affirmative action. Quotas should be illegal. They are not what affirmative action is about.

The difference between "quotas" and "goals and timetables" is twofold. One is semantic, the other is substantive. The semantic difference is about how the terms are defined, while the substantive difference relates to how the terms are used. "Quotas" are restricting and exclusive, used to impose rigid caps on educational and employment opportunities. "Goals and timetables" are flexible and inclusive, designed to achieve fairness only when circumstances and conditions warrant. The difference is significant. Those who oppose affirmative action tend to see it as a quota that effectively caps or limits the number of persons like themselves who can be considered for a particular position or opportunity. Those who favor affirmative action and perhaps belong to a group that has historically been discriminated against tend to see it as an opening, an opportunity for a minimum level of participation.

The medical school had misinterpreted and misapplied the true intent of affirmative action.

Ten years after the Bakke case, the university adopted race- and gender-based considerations for hiring, promotion, and admissions in an attempt to boost the representation of those who had in the past been screened out by existing standards. But in July of 1995, Republican Governor Pete Wilson and the Republican-dominated Board of Regents, in an effort to jump-start Wilson's presidential bid, scored a victory for conservatives everywhere by voting to end racial and gender preferences in the nine-campus UC system, over fierce objections from university officials, students, and professors. And in November of 1996, moreover, the people of California are expected to vote on the so-called California Civil Rights Initiative (CCRI), which, if passed, would repeal affirmative action in public education, public employment, and public contracting.

Wilson, of course, boasted about how he abolished a major affirmative action program; in response, his rivals for the GOP presidential nomination tried to out-*race* Wilson. Senator Phil Gramm tried to attach an anti-affirmative action amendment to a Senate spending bill, and Bob Dole promised to introduce a bill ending all federal preferences. What happens in California can cast a very long shadow on the nation—especially in a presidential election year cycle. Indeed, a conservative group in Colorado now seeks to place on their November 1996 ballot "The Colorado Equal Opportunity Initiative," practically a carbon copy of the CCRI.

Interestingly, the big winners at Berkeley in this "Take back America" movement are not Whites but Asian Americans. Already the leading ethnic group within the student body at Berkeley with 42 percent, they could constitute more than *half* the class in 1997 if restrictions on their admittance are lifted. Whites would benefit very little, perhaps raising their percentage of the student body from 30 percent to 34 percent. Computer analyses project that Black students at the university would drop from 6.4 percent of the class to 1.4 percent and Latinos from 15.3 percent to 5.6 percent. Said *Newsweek,* "Most angry White parents will still be angry."

One has to ask of the Right then: What is the real purpose of this exercise? To alter the UC system to benefit every group other than Black or Latino students? Or is it a tacit effort to use affirmative action as a wedge to divide and conquer people of color?

I think it is both.

There is little question in my mind that the Right seeks to "divide" people by race. The fact is, across America, I'm hard-pressed to think of any group that has not gained as a result of affirmative action, and more generally, the civil rights movement. Latinos. Native Americans. Women. Gays and lesbians. Environmentalists. Animal rights activists. You name it. Black America forced open the door, and everyone else walked on through.

Black America pioneered the opening up of America to all groups who have been socially, politically, or economically disenfranchised. Yet today, affirmative action is being used to turn America against African Americans who are fighting over their already small piece of an ever-shrinking economic pie.

The Right will stop at nothing to turn the clock backward and return society at large to the mythical "good old days," when America seemed racially homogeneous and issues of race were pushed under the carpet. They talk of a color-blind society, but what they mean is an America in which African Americans and other persons of color are virtually invisible.

The attack on affirmative action and other corrective programs that seek to remedy past discrimination and programs that benefit minorities, the poor, the elderly, and the needy represent a vicious assault on fifty years of social and legal reform in this country. The war that's being waged by the radical Right has far worse consequences than the twelve years under Reagan and Bush. Newt Gingrich and the seventy-three Republican freshmen in the House of Representatives are not just touting supply-side economics, but supply-side economics while snatching away the social safety net. Supply-side economics and the trickle-down theory don't work. A rising tide may lift all boats, but only if you have a boat, and most of us don't, much less the kind of luxury yachts favored by the Republican elite.

Ronald Reagan once called the earned income tax credit the best antipoverty program in history. Only families who earn less than $28,000 annually qualify. Yet the Right now wants to cut the earned income tax credit and the low-income housing credit. They want to do away with the Minority Business Development Agency and reduce our investment in education across the board, from Head Start to affordable college loans.

I fear that the Right sees many among us as a permanent underclass. They want to punish the poor just for being poor. They want to deny us the American dream. What about our country's promise of life, liberty, and the pursuit of happiness? Too many of us have been arbitrarily written off by the Right and that is why they've decided to pull the plug on programs that help the less fortunate.

Is affirmative action still needed? The Glass Ceiling Report, sponsored by President George Bush and congressional Republicans, revealed that in the nation's largest companies, only six-tenths of one percent of senior management positions are held by African

Americans. Hispanic Americans make up four-tenths of a percent and Asian Americans a mere three-tenths. Women hold between 3 percent and 5 percent of these positions. The fact is that White males make up 43 percent of our workforce but hold 95 percent of these jobs.

In July 1995, the Chicago Federal Reserve Bank reported that Black home loan applicants are more than twice as likely to be denied credit as Whites with the same qualifications, and that Hispanics are more than one and a half times as likely to be denied loans as Whites with the same qualifications.

The Right has blamed affirmative action for taking away "their" jobs and destroying America's economic vitality.

If that is true, then why does private industry, posting record profits at home, send more and more American jobs abroad?

And why do the wealthiest 2 percent of Americans keep getting richer while tax shelters and tax credits for the middle class and working poor are taken away?

The Right places the blame for our country's ills on people of color, women, the poor, the elderly, the needy, the homeless, the underemployed, and the unemployed, simply because it's convenient. It's so much easier to blame someone else than it is to accept responsibility and try to find new solutions.

In the process, conservatives are attacking the very segment of the American workforce needed to stimulate the U.S. labor market and increase our global competitiveness. We don't have a single person to waste. Every American must be given the educational and economic opportunity to become a contributing member of the U.S. workforce. How else will we ever again become the world's number one manufacturer of goods?

My greatest fear, given the nature and the tone of the national debate about affirmative action, is that we may never get there. Too many people see affirmative action not as a positive force but rather as a guilt-ridden liberal response to America's long, sordid history of discrimination. Too many people think affirmative action coerces employers to hire or promote unqualified minorities. Too many people see affirmative action as nothing more than reverse discrimination.

As a member of the varsity debate team at Indiana University, I learned very early on that half of the battle in any contest is defining the terms of the debate and setting the parameters for discussion. And, as is too often the case, we have allowed the Right to set the tenor of the current debate about affirmative action. The affirmative action debate is not about *reform* but about *repeal*.

Conservatives do not intend to compromise on the issue of affirmative action. We've given them carte blanche to define the debate and set the boundaries. Consequently, every poll, study, and survey in America has found that most Americans are opposed to quotas, racial preference, group rights, special privileges, and, of course, reverse discrimination.

It's time to aggressively fight back, by painting for America a more accurate picture of what affirmative action is and what it is not. In a CNN/*Time* magazine poll, Americans, by 65 percent to 24 percent, favored

President Clinton's policy of "Mend it, but don't end it" when the President had a chance to reeducate the country about the spirit and the purpose of affirmative action.

I believe that the Right has so effectively distorted and soured the national discourse about affirmative action that most Americans need to be reminded that affirmative action's only goal is equal opportunity for all Americans.

Apparently, at least one member of the Supreme Court is even confused about what affirmative action means. Justice Clarence Thomas said, "If I write racism into the law, then I am, in God's eyes, no better than they are. You cannot embrace racism to deal with racism."

What's particularly ironic is that Thomas benefited from affirmative action at various points throughout his life. His very nomination to the Supreme Court is a form of affirmative action. Does anyone really believe that Thomas would have been nominated by George Bush to fill a seat on the court left vacant by anyone other than Thurgood Marshall?

Justice Harry A. Blackmun understood fully why affirmative action is necessary and makes for good public policy. Said Blackmun, "In order to get beyond racism, we must first take account of race. There is no other way. And in order to treat some persons equally, we must treat them differently."

Affirmative action reviews, sponsored by both Republicans and Democrats, find that women, along with Blacks, Latinos, and other persons of color, earn considerably less than their White male counterparts, provided they even have a job. Although women, for example, make up nearly half of America's workforce, they earn less pay than men for jobs requiring the same skills. Women with college degrees earn, on average, only slightly more than men with high school diplomas, according to the U.S. Labor Department.

In 1994 alone, the federal government received more than ninety thousand complaints of employment discrimination based on race, ethnicity, or gender. Less than 3 percent were for so-called reverse discrimination.

There is no statistical or empirical data which suggests or even hints that affirmative action has done anything other than allow for a more diversified and qualified American labor force.

Affirmative action has helped move more people of color into the middle class, thus bridging the economic gap between all groups, and consequently strengthening the overall U.S. economy.

And yet somehow, despite all the evidence to the contrary, the Left finds itself in what can only be described as a dogfight to save a program that has been the vehicle for removing the effects of discrimination.

BENEFITS FROM AFFIRMATIVE ACTION

The opponents of affirmative action, who have dominated the debate thus far, would have us believe that corrective programs are no longer needed in America, that inequality and discrimination are in America's past. They argue that the chief benefactors of affirmative action have been Black Americans, who need to stop whining and get jobs.

I don't get the impression that African Americans are whining about anything. I think that Black folks, like most Americans, are feeling the pain of a tight economic job market. But African Americans, as every statistic shows, are the ones who feel the most pain.

So often we hear people say that Black folks don't have a work ethic. It seems to me that if, in fact, the American work ethic has been killed, what destroyed it was not laziness on the part of Blacks or anyone else. It was minimum wage jobs that people can't afford to live on, let alone raise a family on.

The winners after twenty-five years of affirmative action are not exclusively Black people. It is abundantly clear that women, especially White women, have benefited greatly as well. And when they take advantage of affirmative action, so do their spouses and their kids.

Bottom line: A great many have been affirmative action winners.

WHO LOSES?

Really, no one. In fact, all of society gains. The fact is that, in terms of "set-asides"—where the government sets aside a certain portion of any contract for minorities and women to bid on—on average, 85 percent to 90 percent of all contracts go to White companies. That leaves a mere 10 percent to 15 percent for women and persons of color.

So how are White men being hurt? They receive 90 percent of the economic pie. Yet when a White contractor ends up not winning a bid, he wants to blame the minority- or woman-owned or -managed company for his loss.

The same is true in higher education. When White college students do not get into Harvard or Yale, they blame a person of color for having taken their seat in the classroom. I find it odd that the first person they want to blame is the individual least represented in the class. What about the 80 percent to 90 percent of White students in the classroom?

Believe it or not, there are other factors that are vitally important to getting into school or landing a job. Factors that better speak to future success than mere test scores or grades; things like motivation, determination, and hard work. The fact that candidates of color may not have had the same high quality of education or training often says less about their abilities but far more about their circumstances. Economic and social hardships that, for many, teach the values of perseverance and self-reliance firsthand. Additionally, a good many White students entering Ivy League institutions, for example, attend private schools where they receive special tutoring in preparing for the SAT, and not infrequently, have a natural affirmative action advantage, in that their parents are alumni. This is one of those hidden forms of affirmative action to which no conservative would ever voice opposition. And nonracial preferences don't just cover children of alumni.

The fact is, by increasing diversity within their student bodies, schools can promote equal access to educational opportunities and provide a broader and more enriched educational experience for all.

WHY SHOULD AFFLUENT BLACK AMERICANS BENEFIT FROM AFFIRMATIVE ACTION?

Believe me, the playing field isn't level, even when affluent Black Americans play the game.

I have a friend who works with a major restaurant chain. We talk almost daily. I have heard countless stories from him about the racism and discrimination he has been subjected to by the corporation he works with. And he's a franchisee!

John H. Johnson, one of the most successful magazine publishers in the nation today *(Ebony* and *Jet),* still has trouble getting the same advertising dollars for his publications that his competitors, aimed at White audiences, get regularly. It's telling, I think, even today, that assumptions about Black people can be more powerful than a lifetime of achievement. Here's but one example. Johnson, while in Washington to attend a White House state dinner, was waiting with his wife for his limousine driver to pick him up at the hotel when he was mistaken as someone's driver. Yet he was standing under the awning in his tuxedo and his wife was wearing a formal gown.

Willie Brown, currently the mayor of San Francisco, once went to look at a condo in San Francisco that he was interested in purchasing. He called ahead and made an appointment to view the property. When the White owner found out that Willie Brown was Black, the condo was suddenly no longer for sale. Brown, disturbed by the sudden change of heart, had one of his staffers, a White female, go over to the condo, and this time, the owner couldn't move fast enough to make a deal.

At the time, Brown was the speaker of the state assembly, the second most powerful man in California government. And this didn't happen in the 1950s but the 1990s, in San Francisco, one of the most liberal cities in the country.

So to say well-to-do Black folks are immune from prejudice and discrimination just isn't true. Their blood may be red, their cash may be green, but their skin is still black.

While some wealthy African Americans may benefit directly from certain affirmative action programs regarding the establishment of minority businesses, the net effect is that thousands of working-class Black Americans benefit indirectly when the owners hire people to run and staff their business enterprises. Studies indicate that not just African Americans but women, the disabled, and other persons of color benefit as well.

Clearly, this should not be seen as a Black versus White fight.

AFFIRMATIVE ACTION COMPROMISES QUALITY

Wrong.

I certainly do not want a lessening of standards to accommodate African Americans, other persons of color, or women. A less than qualified workforce does not benefit any of us, especially as America struggles to regain its position as the world's leading manufacturer.

If my house is on fire, I want the most qualified

firefighter around—Black, Brown, Yellow, or Red, male or female. If there's a burglar trying to break into my bedroom window, I want the most qualified and proficient officer on the force.

What affirmative action does is allow U.S. employers to consider an array of factors beyond standard qualifications, like workforce diversity and gender in the hiring and promoting of all candidates. Affirmative action ought not to be a synonym for unqualified. That bastardizes what affirmative action is all about, and leads to further stereotyping.

The fact is that Whites hold most of the coveted jobs and, consequently, even those who are trying to be fair and unprejudiced hire people they feel comfortable with. The "good-old-boy network" leads to the hiring of more Whites, whether or not they are the best-qualified for the job and regardless of whether their presence will enhance employee diversity. This explains why White guys are still having all the fun. White men account for 43 percent of the workforce (41 percent of the population), own 64 percent of the nation's businesses, and have most of America's best-paying jobs.

According to the U.S. Census Bureau, White men account for:

- 70 percent of all judges.
- 73 percent of all lawyers.
- 75 percent of all police detectives and supervisors.
- 94 percent of all fire company supervisors.
- 95 percent of all senior managers.

This is why I reject the notion of "reverse discrimination." Anyone who finds employment as a result of affirmative action must first be qualified, and no person in this country ought to be hired simply because of his or her race.

DOES AFFIRMATIVE ACTION STIGMATIZE BLACKS?

Although I hate this argument, I must concede there is some truth to the fact that many Blacks in this country have been stigmatized and otherwise tainted by affirmative action in a negative way.

As long as people feel that affirmative action means that employers must hire or promote unqualified employees, quite naturally there's going to be that stigma attached to it. Yet it's interesting to note that the individuals making the argument that Black people are stigmatized by affirmative action usually aren't African Americans. They're White men. The very folks on the Right who want to deny creating equal opportunity for African Americans and others are the ones telling Black folks that affirmative action stereotypes them.

I guess we should thank them for their concern.

What this is really about is doing away with a program that is a proven performer. Again, I am against rigid quotas—but that is never what affirmative action was ever meant to be. Affirmative action has helped to give minorities and women a better hand in a game that for too long was stacked against them. Mainstream America has benefited from its own kind of affirmative action for two hundred years. Affirmative action for women and minorities helps to balance the scales.

AFFIRMATIVE ACTION IS THE CAUSE
OF AMERICA'S ECONOMIC PROBLEMS

Never before in the history of this nation have we so cavalierly blamed those at the bottom of the ladder for the economic condition of our country. In no way is affirmative action the cause of the economic problems which we now face.

Black Americans still lag far behind Whites in every leading economic indicator category, with an unemployment rate about twice that of Whites. The Hispanic rate is even higher. Women still make only 72 percent as much as men do for comparable jobs.

Whatever our economic problems, affirmative action is not to blame. Maybe we should place the blame on jobs going abroad or on an obsolete tax system that favors the wealthy: NAFTA or GATT. But it's certainly not affirmative action.

AFFIRMATIVE ACTION IS FLAWED

Of course it is. "Affirmative action," says President Clinton, "has not always been perfect, and affirmative action should not go on forever. It should be changed now to take care of those things that are wrong, and it should be retired when its job is done. But the evidence suggests, indeed screams, that that day has not come."

There's no such thing as a perfect public policy. If we were going to throw out every public policy in this country that doesn't work in a perfect fashion, we would be left without a single law on the books. Ostensibly, political discourse is for debating the issues and formulating the fairest policy that results in the greatest good. And that's precisely what affirmative action does.

In the affirmative action debate, what we ought to be doing is to reform the program, to make it work better and fairer in the areas where it is wanting. But ultimately, it is a program that brings diversity, health, and vigor to the American workplace, and provides opportunity for those who have historically been left out in the cold.

6

For Black Folks Only

ON BLACK MEN

Here are a few telling statistics taken from the October 1993 issue of *Emerge* about Black men in America today:

- There are 14 million African American males. One-third of young Black men under the age of thirty are in prison, on probation, or on parole.
- Black teenage males are the most likely victims of crime.

- Unemployment for Black males (ages sixteen to sixty-four) is 8.8 percent, almost double that of working-age White males.
- Roughly 14 percent of Black males drop out of high school, compared with 8 percent of White males. About 45 percent of White males who graduate from high school go on to college, compared with just 30 percent of Black males.
- Black men earn seventy-two cents for every dollar earned by White men.
- The life expectancy for African American males (sixty-six years) is seven years less than it is for White males. Black men in Harlem have less chance of living past the age of forty than men in Bangladesh, one of the world's poorest countries.

African American males have become the most feared and maligned group in American society, especially young Black males between the ages of sixteen and twenty-five. But these numbers reveal only one facet of the story, and too often, the numbers themselves just aren't true. Conventional wisdom, for example, says that there are more Black men in prison than there are in college. That is quite a stretch from the truth. A recent study showed 136,000 Black males aged eighteen to twenty-four in prison, compared to 378,000 Black males in the same age bracket enrolled in college.

On the other hand, Black men make up a disproportionately high percentage of America's armed forces, accounting for 30 percent of all men in the Army. Yet the National Opinion Research Center found that 51 percent of all Americans thought Black people were less patriotic than Whites. Again, only one aspect of the "facts" on Black men is being told.

ON BLACK WOMEN

On the other side of the coin, here are a few equally disturbing facts about Black women reported by Farai Chideya in her recent book *Don't Believe the Hype.*

- The majority of Black children are born to single mothers. In 1990, 67 percent of Black children were born to unmarried women.
- A Black female-headed household earns roughly $11,956 annually, while a White female-headed household earns about $20,130 a year.
- There are 1.2 million Black women among the working poor, earning incomes below the poverty level (about $7,000 for an individual, $14,000 for a family of four).
- The average family on welfare consists of a woman and two young children; and 39 percent of the families receiving welfare are Black.
- The life expectancy for Black women (seventy-four years) is six years less than that of White women (eighty years).

Although, thankfully, Black college-educated women have made such financial strides since 1980 that many now earn as much or slightly more than White women with similar education and similar work experience, the consequences for Black America as a whole are significant.

For starters, I sometimes get the sense that all of the attention being focused on the remarkable successes of more visible college-educated Black women is somehow causing us to forget or ignore the many problems of the larger number of poor Black women. (The reverse is true for Black men. The illegal activities of a relative few Black men overshadow the efforts and worthy contributions of the many.) While the headlines read: "Black Women Earn More Than Black Men, Study Finds," Black women still make up a disproportionate number of welfare recipients, still lack access to quality health care, still lead the nation in the number of unplanned and unwanted pregnancies, and many are still subjected to sexual harassment in the workplace while they struggle to raise a family on poverty-line wages.

Second, many White employers favor Black women over Black men because they are both Black *and* female, thus simplifying their effort at diversity in the workplace. Increasingly, Black men find themselves losing out to Black women for employment opportunities, further widening the wage gap between Black women and Black men. The sad irony, according to noted University of Chicago sociology professor William Julius Wilson, is that: "Better-educated Black women face a real dilemma. Do they remain single or do they marry down? All the surveys reveal that people tend to marry within their own class and social circles. One outcome could be not intraracial marriages but more interracial marriages."

As if Black America doesn't have enough to deal with already, the disrespect accorded Black men by some shrewd White employers places Black men and women in yet another no-win situation. Clearly, the problems of Black America cannot be addressed or conquered as long as Black women and men either allow themselves to be pitted against each other, or themselves refuse to thoughtfully communicate with each other.

This is why I was particularly disturbed when certain Black women around the country were so vocal in their opposition to 1995's Million Man March because women were not invited to participate. We need to be supportive of each other. There are certain problems in our community that are specific to Black men. Black men need to develop a sense of unity and mutual concern. That doesn't take anything away from Black women and their contribution to our society. But the fact is, Black women cannot stop Black men from killing other Black men. Black women cannot stop Black men from selling and using drugs. Black women cannot stop Black men from abandoning their children. These are problems that Black men—and only Black men—can and must bring to an end.

I didn't feel the march was intended to be sexist—it was an opportunity for Black men to stand up and take responsibility for our shortcomings. To commit to doing better by ourselves, by our families, and by the African American community at large. There was no outcry earlier in 1995 over the international women's conference in China that brought together women of all colors, classes, and political persuasions from all over the world. No one complained that men were not invited to attend. Nor should we have—it was a positive step.

The distortions, half-truths, and misrepresentations about Black Americans are many. For one thing, the American media tolerates and subsequently perpetuates stereotypes about African Americans. Before long, perception becomes reality. In *Don't Believe the Hype,* Farai Chideya points out five different reasons for the media's distortions:

1. Journalism is one of the most segregated professions in America.
2. Journalists and others in the media are human— they work from what they know. And most journalists are White.
3. It's easy to get stories from the ghetto; it's harder to find the same kind of "interesting" stories in middle-class Black neighborhoods.
4. White journalists are presumed to be objective; Black journalists quite often are presumed not to be objective about racial issues.
5. Once something becomes "conventional wisdom," even if it's misleading, it gets repeated over and over again.

According to Northwestern University professor Robert Entman, African Americans are almost always shown as either news sources or as victims in network TV news coverage. Some 46 percent of stories involving Black people showed them as criminals or as victims of crime, poverty, and discrimination or, as his 1994 study puts it, "as threats to or noncontributing members of

American society." In all, he found nearly 60 percent of network news about Black people was negative.

Unfortunately, one reason for the negative portrayal of African Americans by the media is that sometimes we give them a little too much to work with. It's up to Black men and women to stand up and turn back the tide of negativism against them. No one else can speak up for us.

With seven younger siblings, I have a vested interest in seeing Black people being portrayed more positively in the future. Although I don't have all the answers, I do know only too well the questions that we have all asked as Black folks in America.

WHAT'S WRONG WITH WHITE PEOPLE?

This is probably the question most asked by Black men and women today when they are not in the company of Whites. "So many White brothers and sisters are living in a state of denial in terms of how deep White supremacy is seated in their culture and society," Harvard professor and social critic Cornel West has said. "Now we recognize that, in a fundamental sense, we really do live in different worlds."

Although it disturbs me to say so, there are in fact two very different Americas: one Black, the other White. And the disparity between the perceptions of each has never been more evident than it was during the O. J. Simpson trial. Most Black people hoped he would go free but feared he would not. Most Whites assumed he was guilty. Many Black people felt that, at least in this case, the jury system worked. Most Whites felt the jury system had betrayed them.

How could Blacks and Whites reach such diametrically opposed conclusions to the O. J. Simpson verdict? Simple. Too many either did not understand or would not accept the fact that the American jury system is predicated on the idea that different people can view the same evidence and reach different conclusions. Every juror must view the evidence and render his or her own conclusion. That's the way our system works, and it happens every day.

The impugning of the jury by White commentators, writers, and other opinion makers—not to mention the White public at large—was disturbing for all of Black America. Is it acceptable to suggest that because the jurors were mostly people of color, primarily from the inner city, and not college-educated, that they were stupid? That they were incapable of assessing guilt or innocence?

Nonsense.

The world is full of educated fools. We work with them every day. Moreover, how many of those who complained about the jury and its verdict have wiggled out of jury duty themselves? If you're going to whine about the dumbing down of the jury system, at least do your time.

The reaction of Robert Shapiro, the acknowledged architect of the Simpson defense team, who publicly denounced his partners, Johnnie Cochran and F. Lee Bailey, over Cochran's use of the "race card," was particularly distressing. Cochran's job, of course, was to win an acquittal for his client. If Simpson had been

Jewish and a police officer involved in the case had a long history of anti-Semitism, I don't think Shapiro would have hesitated to play the "religion card."

Apparently, a verdict of guilty was the only verdict White America would accept. Our criminal justice system, on balance, has worked rather well for two hundred years. Yet now, given the verdict in one racially tinged, celebrity-driven case, our system of jurisprudence is deemed fundamentally flawed and needs to be completely overhauled. Did the pundits so claim when William Kennedy Smith was acquitted of rape in Florida? Or is it only now true because the celebrity who was acquitted is a Black man?

At no level in our society do Black men compete equally with White men, except on the track, on the field, on the court, or in the ring. So why does White America seem to have its finger pointed at us all the time, the Black community asks? Racism may be our burden, but it is all of America's problem. White America, too, must learn how to overcome it. America runs from the race question simply because people are scared to deal with it. The simple truth is that mainstream America is afraid of Black Americans. And that fear is born mostly out of ignorance. But we run at our own peril. Ask any professional on human behavior and they will tell you that the only way to confront fear is to tackle it head-on.

HOW DO I GET MINE?

Unfortunately, playing by the rules doesn't always get you what you want. Sometimes the most qualified person is passed over time and again simply because of his or her race, gender, or religion. Complaining about it to your friends may make you feel a little better but won't necessarily get you anywhere. Sometimes you just have to be bold, walk into your boss's office, and ask for whatever it is you desire. You may or may not get the promotion, but there's a certain sense of relief in at least saying what's on your mind.

There is a certain risk in this approach. But if we never ask, we're going to keep getting passed over. Isn't it better to at least know where we stand?

In his book *The Rage of a Privileged Class: Why Do Prosperous Blacks Still Have the Blues?*, *Newsweek* correspondent Ellis Cose found that the most disaffected group of people in this country aren't necessarily poor Blacks but the Black middle class. Why? They played by the rules and still reach a point where they can't go any higher. They can look up and see the folks in the executive suite—without hope of ever getting there.

The obstacles that some Black Americans face are so mammoth that sometimes there seems to be no option at all. Too many turn to making a quick buck by selling drugs or engaging in some other illegal activity. Sooner or later, their life, like a house of cards, comes crashing down. There is no shortcut on the path to success.

Sometimes you have to create your own opportunity. If you feel you've earned it, you asked for it and they turned you down, you have no other choice but to take it.

Working in Los Angeles for Mayor Tom Bradley, I was known around the office as an ambitious, aggressive young guy who was always pushing to get ahead.

The others like me were perceived as real "go-getters," men and women on their way up. But I was seen as an opportunist.

Though Bradley was Black, most of his top staffers were not. L.A.'s Black population is only 11 percent, and to keep getting reelected, Bradley couldn't be perceived as a "Black mayor." As a result, he was sensitive to having a multiracial staff.

Realizing that I had reached a glass ceiling, I decided to run for City Council. The councilwoman for my district was antigrowth and had turned down a major economic opportunity for our community. IKEA, the furniture retail outfit, was interested in building a location in the Baldwin Hills/Crenshaw area, which has a predominately Black population. But because her constituents in the other areas of her district, such as Venice and Westchester, which were mostly White, were opposed to growth, she fought to keep IKEA out. We needed that kind of development to bring jobs and economic investment to the community. Unfortunately, she didn't spend enough time communicating with all of her constituents to understand our need.

I saw an opportunity and seized it, running against the incumbent councilwoman. Although I lost a tough race, I did help to make the councilwoman more sensitive to the economic interests of the community. After the campaign, I had two options. I could go back to the mayor's office or create a new opportunity for myself. I decided to break new ground, and thus "The Smiley Report," my daily social commentary on Los Angeles radio, was born.

Nobody gave that opportunity to me. I developed

the concept, I got the advertisers, I sold it to a Black radio station.

I earned it. I asked for it. And finally, I took it. Sometimes that's what we all have to do.

IF RACISM IS A LEARNED BEHAVIOR, WHY DO WE KEEP TEACHING IT?

The great poet Zora Neale Hurston once said, "I remember the very day when I became colored."

No one is born a racist. Nobody comes into this world hating. All children play together in the schoolyard. So if racism is a learned behavior, why do we keep teaching it to our kids?

One of the things I love about New York City and dislike about my own beloved Los Angeles is that practically everyone in New York is forced to interact with other people—on the street, on the bus, on the subway, and in the workplace. Throughout most of America, people are rarely obliged to associate with persons of another race, color, creed, class, or ethnicity except when being served in a restaurant, hotel, or store.

One of the advantages that Bill Clinton has as a President is that he was raised in a community where Blacks associated with Whites, not just worked for them. He didn't have the kind of racism taught to him that many before him had. As a result, he appointed more Blacks as key officials for his Administration than any other President in history. Two of the strongest speeches that Clinton delivered during his first term were in support of affirmative action and reviewing race relations. Clinton felt passionately about these issues because throughout his childhood and his adult life, he learned to understand and appreciate racial and cultural diversity. Unlearning racism will require many more enlightened White Americans to boldly speak out against discrimination and racial injustice.

My hope is that my generation—the so-called Generation X—and the one behind us will do a better job of unlearning this racism. We have no choice. After all, we have had the benefit of living in the most culturally and ethnically diverse America ever. However, we must be mindful of the changing complexion and condition of racism and ethnic hatred. The bombing in Oklahoma City should remind us that new age extremism can be anticolor as well as antigovernment, and antilaw and order.

One thing is certain. We can no longer afford to be indifferent on the matter of race. We sometimes act as if racism is a given human condition. It is not. The realities of racism can be dealt with. Who says that we have to surrender to the hopelessness of racial animus? Like America itself, racism and hatred in the 1990s is many-hued and multicultural. Consequently, the solution, too, must be multifaceted.

WHAT'S WORSE: BLACK-ON-WHITE CRIME, WHITE-ON-BLACK CRIME, OR BLACK-ON-BLACK CRIME?

When a Black person kills a White person, he gets the death penalty. When a White kills a Black, we riot. But when a Black person kills another Black person, we just shrug our shoulders.

This is sad.

Far too many Black people die at the hands of other Black persons. If this alarming trend continues, solving the problems of Black America won't really matter. We will all be dead.

This homicidal epidemic must be given higher priority on the Black agenda. Black Americans are more likely to be victims of violent crime than other Americans, and more often than not, their attackers are also Black. Did you know that nearly half of all murder victims are Black? And that more Blacks kill each other every year than were killed in the entire sordid history of lynchings in America? We have killed more of our own than the Southern bigots ever did.

Disgraceful.

The Reverend Jesse Jackson has suggested that one solution to Black-on-Black crime would be for witnesses to quit worrying about retaliation and just report the crimes to the police. "If the killers were White, surely the young would report them. We must end the silence. It is not disloyal to the race to tell it. The killers will burn the race up unless those in the neighborhood tell it and stop it."

In big cities and small towns across America, Black jurors do, in fact, convict Black criminals. You rarely hear about it, especially in the aftermath of the O. J. Simpson trial, but it's true. Black-on-Black crime is not out of control because Black jurors refuse to throw the book at them. Black-on-Black crime is an epidemic because Black people—especially Black men—have not put down their weapons and Black witnesses have not yet come forth.

Here's clearly an instance where the finger can't be pointed at the White Establishment. We have to first help ourselves.

ARE WE "WE THE PEOPLE"?

More often than not, "We the People" doesn't ring true for African Americans. How can Black Americans be part of "We the People" when they are continually denied the economic, political, and social opportunities available to the rest of society, when they are harassed by the police and otherwise made to feel like outcasts or second-class citizens in their own country?

Frankly, America's Founding Fathers didn't have Black folks in mind when they wrote the words, "We the People." Back then, African Americans were still thought of as only three-fifths of a person—if that. (Today, coincidentally, we remain only three-fifths of a citizen, economically speaking. U.S. Census Bureau figures show that Black Americans still earn about three-fifths of what Whites do.)

Barbara Jordan once wrote: " 'We the People'; it is a very eloquent beginning. But when the Constitution of the United States was completed on the seventeenth of September, 1787, I was not included in that 'We the People.' " Nonetheless, over the centuries, through amendment, interpretation, nullification, and interposition, we have legally become part of the "We" in "We the People."

But sometimes, although it pains me to say so, Black people themselves still act like the forgotten minority, complaining about "the man" and "the system," yet shunning the very tool most capable of righting the wrongs and injustices to which they are subjected almost daily. How can I say this? White Americans vote. We don't. And that's the bottom line. We have to vote. It's a simple message I preach all the time. Black Americans continue to lose far too many important elections by the simple margin of our absence at the polls. Yet, ironically, Black men, specifically, stand to gain the most by participating in the process. The Million Man March, for example, made an important statement to all of America about our unity and our dissatisfaction with the status quo. But if we really want to get the public's attention, Black men and women together need to march to the polls. We are the ones who allow conservatives like Ronald Reagan and George Bush to be elected by staying home rather than going to the polls. African Americans must vote and participate in the democratic process. Registered Democrats outnumber Republicans almost two-to-one. Yet we lose at the polls. It's voter turnout that makes the difference.

I went on Black radio immediately following the verdicts in the first Rodney King trial to give people a chance to vent their frustrations and express their fears in the aftermath of the verdict. Of course, the favorite target of most of our callers was the all-White jury in Simi Valley who had found the four police officers accused of beating Rodney King nearly to death not guilty. After listening to caller after caller condemn the jury, I finally asked one of my Black male callers whether or not he was registered to vote? "No," he replied. He then went on to ask me what that had to do with Rodney King getting his butt whipped. Of course, the answer is that Black people can complain until they're blue in the face about this and any other jury decision that they happen not to like. But we should understand that only registered voters can serve on a jury. The point is, don't complain about the jury system unless you are a registered voter, and if you are, when the court calls you to serve, don't try to get out of it.

This may sound strange to some of you, but I can't tell you the joy and satisfaction I felt the first time I voted, or for that matter, every time I vote. When I walk out of that booth, at least I know I've had my say. Your vote is your voice.

There are two other pieces of advice I would offer other African Americans. If you have the opportunity and the financial resources, at some point, visit Africa. You can't begin to understand what it means to be part of "We the People" in America until you first understand who you are, where you came from, and the contribution your ancestors have made throughout history.

My first trip to Africa was one of the most profound experiences I've ever had. When you visit the slave castles, where Africans were warehoused after they were abducted from the fields and separated from their families, you are able to get a visible picture of how they were snatched out of their country, taken against their will, indentured as servants, bought and sold into slavery. It humbles you and places your daily struggles in a more perfect light.

Second, every Black American should visit the nation's capital. This probably sounds trivial, but it's not.

Most people don't realize that Washington, D.C., was designed and laid out with the assistance of a Black man, Benjamin Banneker. The image many of us have of the capital is that of an island reserved for powerful and privileged White men. The White House. Capitol Hill. The Supreme Court. The Sunday political discussion shows. Washington reporters. They're nearly all White, even though the city is predominantly Black. I have a friend from South Africa who, during apartheid, visited Washington, D.C., and noted that our capital was like his country; Black people account for the population, but few Whites have all the power.

Even still, in Bill Clinton's Administration, the departments of Energy, Commerce, and Veterans Affairs are all run by African Americans. More than ever, Black people have a stake and vested interest in running the federal government. But it's the sort of thing that won't hit Black Americans until they go to Washington and see it for themselves. It will give them, as it gave me, a sense of pride and accomplishment. A confirmation that this country belongs as much to Black Americans as it does to anyone else. That we truly are "We the People."

Black men and women will only become more convinced of this when they register to vote and participate in the process. Remember, this land is yours and mine—it is for *all* Americans.

DO AFRICAN AMERICAN ROLE MODELS HAVE TO BE PERFECT?

NO.

First of all, most Black athletes and entertainers are *not* role models. Nor is every Black role model an athlete or an entertainer. Talk to most young Black kids and you will discover that typically their role models are people who they know and trust. Parents. Teachers. Clergy. Relatives. And that's the way it should be.

I, for one, was disturbed by the message that was advertised all over the country by Gatorade a few years back with their "Be like Mike" Michael Jordan commercials. The message we must deliver to our youth is not one of trying to be like Michael Jordan, but rather, liking *themselves,* since they will never *be* Michael Jordan. The fact is, a Black child has a one in eight thousand chance of becoming a player in the NBA; and one chance in ten thousand of playing baseball in the major leagues. Why is it then that we make gifted athletes our role models?

A different problem for us created by society at large is the tendency to see any missteps or mistakes by Black celebrities and spokespeople as representative of the race as a whole. Why is it that Elizabeth Taylor can be married nine times, and nobody talks about her many divorces as being indicative of a breakdown in White family values? She's still the queen of Hollywood royalty and her negative qualities are seen as hers alone. Hugh Grant can be caught with his pants down on Sunset Boulevard, but that doesn't mean his actions signify a breakdown in White morality, nor does it prevent him from having a hit movie. But when Michael Jordan, Michael Jackson, or Black politicians from former congressman and now-president of the United Negro College Fund Bill Gray to New York Congressman Floyd Flake are even *accused* of a crime, somehow it's a setback for *our* cause.

Not so. They're human, just like everyone else. I don't know any of these men personally, but what they may or may not do is not a reflection on me or Black Americans generally. We have to stop allowing the media to paint all Black people with this broad brush. And stop feeling guilty when they do. Black role models shouldn't be expected to be any more perfect than White ones are.

Rather than adopting celebrities as role models, each of us would do better to serve as mentors and tutors to Black youth. These are the kind of positive role models our children and our communities need. Mentors and tutors provide the attention and help that our youth are looking for in their lives.

When we get involved with our communities, we take some of the pressure off superstars like Michael Jordan. After all, he's just a very talented athlete. That's it.

WHY THE RAP ON RAP?

Politicians on the Right love to criticize Black rap music. Yet the majority of rap recordings are purchased by White kids—76 percent, in fact. Rap music is an easy target for politicians like Bob Dole and Bill Bennett, because a few artists rap about killing cops and refer to women as "b _ _ _ _ _ _" and "ho's." The fact is, excluding these few extremists, rap is a viable art form.

The First Amendment protects all of us. I don't agree with many of the rappers' messages, but I will defend unto the death their right to say what's on their minds. Were it not for the First Amendment, Martin Luther King, Jr., and all those who fought in the civil rights movement and spoke out against the sorry conditions for Black men and women in America never would have had the right to express themselves. They would have been silenced.

We do, however, need to challenge rap artists to do better by us. There's no excuse for some of their lyrics. As the Reverend Jesse Jackson has noted: "There is also no excuse for our ghettos—where young men can't find jobs nor support families, where hope has gone and drugs and guns become a way out."

Adds writer bell hooks, "Many of those same people who oppose rap in the public sphere are themselves anti-Semitic, misogynist, and homophobic. It's a lie that the conservative forces that are attacking rap really care about those issues."

Still, there's no denying that what started out as a viable art form has become too nasty. The rappers defend their art by saying they just reflect the society that they live in. Isn't that exactly the same thing TV news directors say when we call them on the carpet for their obsession with inner-city crime? We can't have it both ways.

We need to challenge both to be more responsible.

IF I WERE WHITE . . . ?

One of the most common "what-ifs" posed by Black men and women is: "If I were White, I would do . . . I would have . . ."

These statements are troublesome because they give the impression that the only way to achieve success in America is to be White. I'm reminded of the classic movie *Imitation of Life,* in which a young Black woman, in search of success, tries desperately to escape being Black by "passing," only to realize that trying to be something you aren't can have tragic consequences.

I hate how the "If I were White . . ." line plays with young Black boys and girls. We should be *proud* to be Black Americans. Black folks should stop fantasizing about the White way of life being the right way of life and recommit to being the best at whatever we are.

Someone once said, "There are no good times to be Black in America, but some times are worse than others." Being Black in America is not easy. None of us volunteered. But we have shown time and again that self-reliance and self-respect, not color, are what matters.

OUR MOTHERS, SISTERS, GRANDMOTHERS, AUNTS, AND NIECES ARE WOMEN. THEN WHY DO SO MANY BLACK MEN TREAT BLACK WOMEN SO BADLY?

I think Black Americans know why. I just don't think we want to admit it.

Black men treat Black women so badly because most of us have been spoiled to death by our mothers, and given the greater ratio of Black women to Black men in America, we often get away with taking them for granted. Black men must do better.

I have seven younger brothers and my mother supplies them with anything and everything they need. I don't think she's that different from other Black mothers. It's been said about Black mothers: "They love their sons, but they raise their daughters." The implication is that Black boys get away with a lot, while moms keep a tight reign on their girls.

Why? Perhaps because Black mothers have been keenly sensitive to the difficulties Black men face in mainstream America. Remember, one-third of Black men under thirty are in prison, on probation, or on parole. What do Black women do when the numbers of available, loving, kind, caring, and responsible Black men are dwindling? Increasingly, Black women marry outside the Black race. And that's obviously not good for the Black family in the long run.

I'm not arguing against interracial marriage, but I hate to see Black women marry White men by default. That's probably one reason why interracial marriages have tripled since 1970. For too many Black women, there simply aren't enough "desirable" Black men. This stark reality must change.

Many successful Black brothers turn their backs on Black women by wedding White women as well, but for a different reason. Black men have been hoodwinked by Madison Avenue into believing that what's really beautiful in America is a woman with blond hair and blue eyes. This kind of "trophy wife" is a way of marrying up in White society.

The myth that we have bought into that White is right must be overcome. We need to affirm our own intrinsic worth and beauty.

Black women have stood beside, behind, and even before Black men when we were too timid to stand up for ourselves. The time is now to stop disrespecting them. We should be celebrating Black women.

WHAT'S UP WITH THE BLACK CHURCH?

The Black church is the most powerful positive force within the Black community, and it bothers me that, compared to Black women, so few Black men regularly attend. If anything, we ought to be running to church on Sunday.

So many of the problems in Black communities— Black-on-Black crime, out-of-wedlock births, and gang violence—would dramatically decrease if we would just spend a little more time with God. The sooner we return to the embrace of the church, the sooner I believe we will find solutions to our social ills. The Black church was the glue that held the community together through slavery, centuries of discrimination and racism, and the Great Depression. It can now help us to overcome the drugs, violence, poverty, and crime that are so common a denominator in society today.

And although it took them a little while to catch on, in January of 1996, five of the United States' largest African American church denominations announced that they were forming a for-profit organization to pool their resources to provide health insurance, home mortgage loans, credit cards, education, food, and durable goods to Black Americans. It's about time. Together the denominations total forty-three thousand churches and 20 million members.

Booker T. Washington was right. "At the bottom of education, at the bottom of politics, even at the bottom of religion, there must be for our race economic independence."

CAN WE GET IT TOGETHER SO THAT WE CAN GET TOGETHER?

Do we really have a choice? We can only point the finger at "the White man" for so long. I am no longer interested in trying to change White America or blame all of our problems on them. Neither helps us to take our own lives in our hands and move forward.

The thing I most admired about the Million Man March was that, unlike most Washington marches, Black men were not there to petition the government for anything. Nobody was asking for a hand or a handout. Atonement and self-improvement were the themes that Black men heard throughout the day.

The federal government should not be let off the hook for its responsibility to provide work for those who can work, shelter for the homeless, care for the elderly and the infirm, hope for the downtrodden, and a safe and secure America for all.

But, with or without the government, Black America must be determined to do better by ourselves and our people. We've gotten too caught up in maneuvering to land the big corporate job, purchasing the right kind of automobile, wearing the most fashionable designer threads. We've been chasing a materialistic dream, and in the process we've been running from our duty. I wonder what Marcus, Malcolm, Medgar, or Martin would have to say about our priorities?

Moreover, we don't seem to be developing young leadership. Show me a prominent young Black person, and I'll show you someone who is probably known for his or her accomplishment in sports, the arts, or entertainment. Now, I don't begrudge any brother or sister success and wealth. I do, however, recognize that most athletes, artists, and entertainers don't provide much leadership. Excitement, but not empowerment.

We have plenty of complex issues to grapple with. The proliferation of drugs in our communities, the lack of economic opportunity, political apathy, police brutality, and Black-on-Black crime, to name a few.

I fear that the Million Man March and the verdict in the O. J. Simpson case will result in a backlash, or more accurately a "Blacklash" against our community. For every action, there is a reaction. While many in Black America rejoiced at the not-guilty verdict in the Simpson trial and spoke of Black unity around the march, White America was driven to the edge. They were, by and large, upset and confused by the difference in our reactions to the same events. I believe that there will be a quiet White revolt at the polls in November 1996.

White conservatives will attempt to "put down" the "counterculture" by continuing their efforts to eliminate affirmative action; by declaring English the official language; by voting to deny education and health care to our poorest citizens. Of the 38 million people living in poverty in America—some 30.6 percent are African Americans and 30.7 percent are Latinos—over 61 percent of the total number of poor.

Unless we take steps to counteract it, the 1996 election, I fear, will serve as a referendum by the Right against what they perceive as an attack on their way of life. The only way we can avoid the coming Blacklash is to mount a political counterattack against the radical Right by encouraging all African American men and women of voting age to register and turn out at the polls—to ensure that their voices are heard and their votes are tallied.

"The tragedy of life does not lie in not reaching your goal," the educator Dr. Benjamin E. Mays once said. "The tragedy lies in having no goal to reach. Not failure, but low aim is sin."

It's really now or never. We have to set higher goals and get our act together so that we as a people can get together.

7

For "Angry Whites" Only

Seven Things White Conservatives Should Know

In the past two years, the media has often trotted out the image of the "angry White male" to describe the backlash against Blacks, women, and other ethnic groups by conservative White voters. I'm glad that the mainstream media coined this phrase so that my use of the term doesn't obscure or nullify what I'd like to share in this chapter.

Sometimes I wonder whether all those White men who are not conservative are as bothered by being labeled "angry" as I was when, not too long ago, Black men were so commonly lumped together into the monolithic category of the "angry Black male."

It's interesting that a single word, "angry," has been used to describe the two groups of people in America who are most often at odds—conservative Whites and "radical" Blacks. Yet, when the word "angry" is cited to describe Black men, it most often means contrary, out of control, mad, or something of the sort, while the word "angry," when used to describe White men in America, is generally associated more with a justifiable passion to "take back America." I don't rightly know how this happened, but I find it an interesting observation nonetheless. Certainly, the wrath of the "angry White male" in America has been felt. The November 1994 congressional elections sent a resounding message across the country that Middle America was pretty ticked off.

But I'm still not convinced that what happened in November 1994 was a "mandate" for the Right. The fact is, 6 million fewer people voted in 1994 than voted in 1992. So, did the Right have any more of a mandate than Bill Clinton did in 1992? I think not. The Left lost in 1994 because fewer of us made it to the polls. There's a big difference between *voters* and the *electorate*. Nonetheless, conservatives won and that's what counts. I believe their angst is worth noting and addressing.

I think it would be foolish to dismiss the legitimate concerns of decent fair-minded voters, just because a small but vocal group of "angry White men" harbor racial animosity. But it is equally foolish for conservative voters, angry or otherwise, to labor under false assumptions and beliefs about what America was, is, should be, or will become.

Talk radio, television, and my other life experiences as a political aide and social activist have allowed me a chance to become better acquainted with the position of conservative voters. But these same experiences have made me more painfully aware of what the rest of America wants to share with them as well.

Unfortunately, in the world's most culturally and ethnically rich nation, we still talk past or around one another, rather than to each other. And my sense is that conservatives, frightened by the pace of change in America, are the ones most reluctant to dialogue with their opposites about the issues which threaten to tear the very fiber that holds the country together.

Race, human rights, immigration, civil rights, affirmative action, and other important social concerns of the day are urgent and persistent matters that must be talked about—not simply legislated out of existence. Maya Angelou, in her poem "On the Pulse of Morning," which she read at President Clinton's inauguration, put it best when she said that "History, despite its wrenching pain cannot be unlived, but if faced with courage, need not be lived again."

Turning a deaf ear or a blind eye will not make these pressing concerns go away. Not Houdini, not even David Copperfield's greatest illusion could make these matters disappear. Only rational discourse and time can.

SEVEN THINGS EVERY "ANGRY WHITE AMERICAN" SHOULD KNOW

We Feel Your Pain

As I mentioned earlier, since 1960 Blacks on average have earned 60 percent of what Whites have earned—a figure that has held constant despite significant gains in education and hiring of Blacks. On average, Blacks pay half a percentage point more for mortgage rates than Whites. That averages out to $12,000 over the thirty-year life of the median fixed-rate mortgage in the U.S.A. Even so, a Black-owned home similar to a White-owned home is valued $31,000 lower. If houses and vehicles are included, the median Black family's net worth is $8,300, compared with a median White family net worth of $56,000.

As a Black man, living with racism, discrimination, and lost opportunity has given me a pretty good handle on life's injustices. So for those White conservatives who feel threatened by the prospect of having to share a little of their space, I feel their pain. It's something many of us have had to experience for quite a long time.

No Guilt Trip

Bob Dole has used the phrase "elitist guilt" when talking about race relations. Listen, liberals are not trying to lay a guilt trip on conservatives. We're not trying to make White conservatives feel guilty about their status and values.

Affirmative action and other corrective programs are designed to simply level the playing field. It's like stepping into a crowded elevator. We're not asking those inside to get out, just to move over and make room for the rest of us.

No, Whites today weren't responsible for slavery. But they have indirectly benefited from the racial inequality and economic injustice that arose out of it. What Senator Bill Bradley calls "White skin privilege." Now, we must all share in the wealth of America and the opportunity herein.

That's not guilt. That's reality.

We Are Not the Enemy

Life, liberty, and the pursuit of happiness. All Americans, regardless of race, color, creed, gender, religion, or political persuasion, want the same thing. Why does that put people of color at odds with "angry White men"? It shouldn't.

As my mother used to exclaim while my nine siblings and I made a mad dash to the dinner table: "Calm down, there's enough to go around." Sometimes when my mother had cooked one of my favorite meals, I would stuff my face as quickly as possible in order to assure myself of first place in line for seconds. The images of my childhood greed are not dissimilar to America in the 1990s.

Yes, there is enough of America to go around. Despite what political pundits on the Right might say. Isolationism, relativism, protectionism, and greed may symbolize America in the 1990s, but they are so clearly un-American. They run counter to every long-standing American tradition and belief. Some conservatives act as if they alone made America what she is today. For starters, that's not always something to brag about. But second, would America be America without the contributions of all her peoples? Of course not.

Liberal Americans are not the enemy. All Black men are not criminals and all Black women are not welfare queens. All Spanish-speaking persons are not gang members or illegal aliens. All organizations that resist prayer in the schools are not anti-Christian. All women who fight sexism are not "femi-nazis."

The only way to bring this nation together is to talk about the things that unite us, as well as the things that divide us. This is especially true following the O. J. Simpson trial. Trying to bridge our differences can be painful for all of us. But too many Americans live segregated lives. They don't put themselves in situations where they can both share and learn from persons of another race, economic class, or even gender.

Consequently, whatever hostilities, differences of opinions, or fears we've been carrying around, we just keep on carrying around. And like the Energizer bunny, our mutual distrust just keeps going and going.

Let's face it. It is patently unfair to blame any particular ethnic group, gender, or religious group for the state of our nation. Where we fall short, it is the responsibility of us all. We all feel a sense of frustration, and there is much to be done.

We feel America's pain. But we are not the **enemy.** We are the **energy.**

No U-Turn

The Right seems determined to "reclaim" America by any means necessary. Even if it means returning our nation to the racism, sexism, segregation, and discrimination that permeated decades past. I'm waiting for the party of Lincoln to re-propose slavery any day now.

We need to expand the opportunities for all Americans, not take a U-turn back to the nineteenth century and the Gilded Age.

It's too late to turn back the clock. At most, progress can be slowed, but it cannot be stopped. Again, we cannot move forward by going backward. Why even try?

The Color of Crime

The great Black writer James Weldon Johnson once said, "Every race and every nation should be judged by the best it has been able to produce, not by the worst." Especially when the worst represents a small percentage of the community at large.

African Americans disproportionately represent both criminals and victims in America. But that is a societal injustice. "Black male" should not be a synonym for "criminal."

Studies have found that, since the beginning of the Reagan Administration in 1980, legislators across the country have adopted laws that, by themselves, tend to unfairly punish African Americans and other poor persons. African Americans are now seven times more likely to go to prison than Whites.

Are Blacks committing more crime or doing more time?

The Sentencing Project study also found that the nation's war on drugs is hurting young Black Americans most by sending them to prison at vastly higher rates than accounted for by their rate of drug use or their percentage of the population. This is primarily because crack cocaine sentencing laws disproportionately affect Black men. As written, the law requires 100 times as much powder cocaine to trigger the same mandatory minimum sentence as crack cocaine. Indeed, the U.S. Sentencing Commission advocates that the sentencing for crack and powder cocaine be equal. The continued erosion of conditions in the nation's inner cities and more intense police attention and focus on these areas have led to this unfortunate and unfair reality.

It is ironic and unfortunate that most violent crime in America today is committed by *young* people. Of all races, colors, creeds, and classes. As a society, we should be trying to deal with the increasing violence at the hands of young people. Too often, we find it much easier to just target Black men.

If crime does have a color, it's usually "green," not Black.

Not Yet

A *USA Today*/CNN/Gallup Poll taken after the verdict found that the O. J. Simpson trial "left white Americans bitter, cynical about the criminal justice system, and overwhelmingly convinced that race relations will worsen as a result."

The survey found that 77 percent of Whites felt the Simpson trial has done more to hurt race relations. More disturbing, 55 percent thought race relations will always be a problem.

My immediate response is to agree with White respondents. After all, if White Americans hold such a pessimistic view about the future of race relations, why wouldn't Blacks feel similarly? It takes two to tango.

But in my heart, I remain hopeful that the debate about race, which we are now engaged in, can be seen as an opportunity for Americans to foster a new racial harmony.

Of one thing, though, I am certain. Now is not the time to start turning our backs on the hard-won social, political, and civil rights gains of the past three decades and retreat to a separate but unequal America.

As I've pointed out earlier in this book, the playing field is not yet level for Black Americans, other persons of color, or women. Racism, discrimination, and sexism are still far too common. The Half-Right, reluctantly, concedes their existence but denies their impact.

Indeed, the *USA Today*/CNN/Gallup Poll found that only 6 percent of White respondents felt racial discrimination against Black people in this country was a "very serious" problem.

This after Rodney King's civil rights were violated by White police officers in Los Angeles. After Mark Fuhrman, in the "trial of the century," was shown to have perjured himself when he testified that he never used the word "nigger." The extent of this L.A. police officer's racism, one who was sworn to protect and serve, indeed shocked the entire nation. This after Malice Green was beaten to death by White police officers in Detroit. And after Charles Stewart in Boston and Susan Smith in South Carolina blamed mystery Black men for crimes they committed and the media and police believed them initially.

To be sure, things are better than they were in decades past. But we're far from being a society of equals.

Contrary to popular belief, the "other" America has not yet arrived.

Do Unto Others as You Would Have Them Do Unto You

What we all learn as children, we shun as adults: treating others as we would like to be treated.

Supreme Court Justice Clarence Thomas claimed that it was "God's law" that required him to vote against affirmative action. Senator Jesse Helms, California Representative Bob Dornan, and others have used the same line on other issues. I believe that most Americans, including those who are deeply religious, strongly support the constitutional doctrine of the separation of church and state. Increasingly, however, we are seeing an inappropriate mixing of politics and religion, thanks to organizations like the Christian Coalition, who claim to speak for American families. Ironically, the Christian Coalition does not speak for people of faith on matters of public policy.

Not a single plank in the Christian Coalition's so-called Contract with the American Family is supported by 60 percent of the American public, according to a nationwide survey of registered voters conducted by Peter D. Hart Research Associates. Voters overwhelmingly oppose the following Christian Coalition proposals:

- They reject vouchers for private and religious schools by a 60 to 35 percent margin.
- They reject the replacement of public assistance with private charity by a 59 to 32 percent margin.
- They reject amending the U.S. Constitution's religious liberty provisions by a margin of 58 to 34 percent.
- They reject the abolition of the Department of Education and the cutting back of education funding by a margin of 57 to 36 percent.
- They reject the abolition of federal support for arts, humanities, public broadcasting by a 55 to 41 percent margin.
- They reject the restriction of abortion and elimination of federal family planning by a margin of 54 to 40 percent.

I know God is many things, but He is not a weapon to be used against those of us who are deeply religious but happen to disagree with the Christian Coalition.

In South Africa, Nelson Mandela governs by the golden rule. He is doing unto others as he would have had them do unto him, which is pretty amazing when you consider that he was forced to spend twenty-seven years in jail for speaking out against a racist regime.

Said Mandela in his 1994 inaugural speech: "We enter into a covenant that we shall build the society in which all South Africans, both Black and White, will be able to walk tall, without any fear in their hearts, assured of their inalienable right to human dignity—a rainbow nation at peace with itself and the world."

Calming, healing words from a President who could have easily engaged in retaliation and reverse apartheid by banishing all the Whites to townships, as the ruling White South Afrikaners had done to the Black natives. But he didn't.

Here in America, conservatives fight against progress because they fear the changing color of America will one day make them the minority. I feel that they, too, fear retaliation and certainly a loss of control.

But that did not happen in South Africa and that will not happen in America. If anybody had a reason to hate, it was Martin Luther King, Jr. He was jailed, beaten, hosed down, and, of course, eventually assassinated. But Dr. King refused to hate. Retaliation, he often said, took too much energy. "Hatred and bitterness can never cure the disease of fear," King once said. "Only love can do that. Hatred paralyzes life; love releases it. Hatred confuses life; love harmonizes it. Hatred darkens life; love illuminates it.''

To this day, my grandmother urges me to "treat everybody right." It's only when you hate that you find yourself thinking up ways to scheme and to deny others opportunity.

Do unto others as you would have them do unto you. It's not just the best policy. It's the only policy.

8

The Next Frontier

The Battleground of the Future

Do you get the sense that the Right is so much better than we are at sniffing out issues that play well to the public?

I sure do.

But I don't believe that the only way to appeal to the American people is through divisive or condescending points of view. Although the Right has shown that carrot-and-stick politics—the carrot of tax cuts and the stick of racial fear—can be effective in the short run, they are dangerously counterproductive to America's long-term future. The blame-somebody-else solutions of the Right must be tolerated no longer.

Doing away with programs that educate and empower our citizens, for example, is not acceptable. Legislation or policies that deny Americans an opportunity to make the best of themselves that they can are never right.

The "Take back America" injunctions of the Right may superficially appeal to Americans afraid for their livelihoods and way of life, but the cynicism and hardheartedness fundamentally at its core will inevitably turn most Americans off, once they see it for what it is.

But the Right, of course, is not limiting their campaign to remake American politics to the current issues of the day—be it abortion, affirmative action, "three strikes" sentencing, or voter registration. Already they are anticipating and setting the stage for the ideological battleground of the future. Here is a sampling of some of the issues which we can expect to be front-line confrontations in the years to come.

THE FLAT TAX

First of all, there really is no such thing as "the" flat tax, only the concept of "a" flat tax. I make this distinction because everyone who supports the idea of a flat tax defines its meaning in a different way. Indeed, any idea which is endorsed by both Jerry Brown and Pat Buchanan, diametrical opposites, is cause for concern and caution. A flat tax may sound simple enough on its surface, but here again the devil is in the details.

Over the next year or two, presidential election debate will result in massive media attention to the idea of a flat tax. Politicians on the Right primarily, spurred by millionaire businessman and GOP presidential hopeful Steve Forbes and led in Congress by House Majority Leader Dick Armey, will try to convince America that a flat tax is simpler, fundamentally fair, would net increased tax revenues for government spending and make our economy the strongest in the world.

I'm not yet personally convinced that a mere flat tax could or would do all that. Like most Americans, however, I do believe that our complex and burdensome system of taxation might well benefit from tax code reform. But tax simplicity should ultimately help renew America, not screw America.

A flat tax that rewards the rich and punishes the middle class by taking away the home mortgage deduction is unacceptable. Such a plan would further hinder Americans trying to buy their first home and consequently have adverse effects on the real estate and construction industries. I'm not impressed by a flat tax that eliminates taxes on capital gains, interest income, and dividends, since most in the middle class don't benefit from such income anyway. Indeed, some in the middle class would end up paying more in taxes, given this provision. And why strip away the value of charitable deductions? And if tax loopholes account for $600 billion in tax revenues lost to the government each year, why not close the corporate loopholes before advocating a questionable flat tax? Furthermore, should a flat tax free up additional revenue for government spending as Republicans claim, are we supposed to believe that the Right will spend that money on policies and programs that benefit the least among us? Please.

Dick Armey has called a flat tax "an idea of great moral force and radical simplicity." Perhaps. But such "radical simplicity" requires much more discussion and debate. The questions—and pitfalls—about a potential flat tax are many, but the answers are few. This is an issue we'll all have to follow closely.

IMMIGRATION

In 1993 (the most recent year for which figures are available), over eight hundred thousand legal immigrants were admitted to the United States, as well as an estimated three hundred thousand illegal immigrants. (Some prefer to use the phrase "illegal alien," but I've never liked that term because it tends to dehumanize such people and make them sound as if they're life-forms from another planet.)

Although I have no scientific evidence to support this, I believe that asking Americans their opinions on U.S. immigration policy is one thing, but asking about the contribution or value of immigrants to our society is quite another. The former is vague and reeks of "us and them." The latter personalizes the issue, making us look into the faces of our friends, neighbors, and coworkers, as opposed to a faceless mass of non-English-speaking foreigners.

Immigration is fast becoming one of the issues around which future political battles will be waged, as it was most recently in the California gubernatorial and U.S. Senate races in 1994. Until now, immigration has only been an issue in border states like California, Texas, and Florida. But California Governor Pete Wilson proved that demonizing immigrants has "political legs" and can help resuscitate a floundering reelection campaign. Early in the campaign, Wilson trailed his Democratic opponent by forty points, yet by riding the wave of antiimmigrant sentiment in California, he soundly bested his challenger. Attacking immigrants apparently works, and I'm certain that we'll be seeing a lot more scapegoating by politicians on the Right.

But this debate must not be framed only as a fight about whether to keep our borders open or to close them. The debate must be foremost about what immigrants—all immigrants—have meant to America. What gets forgotten is that most of us in America came from somewhere else. We are a land of Italians, Jews, Irish, Poles, Chicanos, Africans, Asians, Filipinos, Vietnamese, Chinese, Koreans, and people from every other country of origin you can imagine.

Over the last decade, as many as 10 million legal and illegal immigrants established permanent residence in the United States—a number higher than at any period in our history, including the peak immigration decade of 1900 to 1910. The effect of this trend has pushed so many social hot buttons that a nation of immigrants is now wondering whether it should remain one. Although numbers alone never tell the whole story, it is clear that something must be done to reform U.S. immigration policy.

Recent polls show that 59 percent of Americans feel that immigration was good for the country in the past, but only 29 percent think it is a good thing now. But why is the Right so clearly scapegoating immigrants for political gain? Is there another agenda? Why the intense interest in immigration now? I believe that the spin we've allowed the Right to put on the immigration issue is obscuring their attempt to dodge responsibility for the decline of American industry and quality of life and redirect the blame away from business, our declining education, and our fraying social system toward a group that has no voice and can little defend itself. A congressional commission on immigration led by the late Representative Barbara Jordan recommended in 1995 that *legal* immigration be cut by one-third, a recommendation that President Clinton immediately endorsed. The question is no longer whether immigration reform will occur, but how. Stiff new curbs on immigration are certain. What remains unclear is how far the Right is willing to push to force the country to turn its back on a revered and invaluable American tradition.

Do we cut off federal funding to local governments that do not cooperate with the capture of illegal immigrants? Establish a worker identification program? Deny immigrants eligibility for public benefits (which, apart from education, only the elderly and refugees take advantage of anyway)? Pass a constitutional amendment to deny citizenship to children born in the United States to illegal immigrants, even though the Constitution currently provides that all people born in the United States are U.S. citizens, regardless of their parents' status? Place a moratorium on *legal* immigration?

One of the things I find most troubling in this debate is that the line between "legal" and "illegal" immigration has become so blurred. Legal immigration is what has helped make America what she is today. It is uncontrolled illegal immigration that threatens her future. But it ought to be dealt with at the federal government level in a firm, sensible, and nonpartisan way. "Immigrant" has become a code word for unwanted foreigners—usually anyone of a different color, speaking another language, who will, in the eyes of the Right, drain rather than benefit our society, and whom our tax dollars will have to subsidize. Whether the immigrant is here legally or illegally is a distinction that is becoming less and less important.

It is true that 97 percent of immigrants who came here one hundred years ago were European or Canadian. By contrast, in 1993, about 80 percent of legal immigrants were from Spanish-speaking, Asian, African, and Caribbean countries. Just a few countries dominated the stream: Nearly 40 percent of all immigrants came from Mexico, China, the Philippines, Vietnam, and the Dominican Republic.

When I hear politicians on the Right such as Pat Buchanan talk about "social cohesion" and the like, I can't help but wonder whether what he's really complaining about is the way these figures are already starting to shift the racial balance of our nation.

The U.S. Census Bureau projects that, by the year 2050, the majority of the U.S. population will become non-White. Is it any wonder that Buchanan and others are blaming immigration policy for this unspeakable horror? What were once private mutterings are now, in the context of immigration, rather bold public pronouncements.

But the melting pot of old continues with today's new immigrants. While the majority of immigrants admitted to the United States these days are non-Whites, intermarriage rates in the United States have never been higher; nor have mixed-race births. According to the Population Reference Bureau, births to mixed Japanese-White couples now exceed those to all-Japanese couples. About half of all American Jews marry non-Jews. One-third of young U.S.-born Hispanics marry non-Hispanics. Nearly half of all Hispanics consider themselves White.

There are now so many ethnically mixed persons in the United States that apparently the Census Bureau is debating about whether or not to create a special classification for them.

Buchanan says, "The twenty-five million who have come in here in the past twenty years have to be acculturated and assimilated." Well, as best I can tell, immigrant assimilation is going on.

And as for the contention that hardworking Americans have to subsidize new immigrants, *The Los Angeles Times* estimates that, of the roughly 4 million illegal immigrants in the United States, 3 million are employed. One-third of them work as domestics. That's a 75 percent employment rate, doing work that most of us flatly refuse to even consider.

I once had a caller on radio who complained that illegal immigrants were taking jobs away from Americans who needed work. I asked the caller whether he really wanted to nanny babies, bus tables, wash or park cars, cook, or pick grapes all day, or sell oranges and bananas on the local freeway overpass.

Anyone who's studied U.S. immigration policy—as opposed to engaging in mere political pandering—knows that race or ethnicity is not the problem with regard to immigration. Greater efforts to curb legal immigration will not solve the real problem of illegal immigration and enforcing laws already on the books against it.

The problem with legal immigration, according to the experts, is that our policy is based more on family kinship than marketable job skills. Overall, more than half the 1993 immigrants of working age reported low-skilled or unskilled occupations. Almost two-thirds of immigrants were admitted solely because they were related, either closely or in an extended fashion, to someone already here. This fact is borne out by the nation's immigrant clusters. Between 1991 and 1993, selected ZIP codes in New York City, Los Angeles, Chicago, Miami, and Houston together averaged 206,000 new immigrants a year. Most of those were extended family members.

The suggestion that immigrants come here not to work, but for government largesse, is without merit. Many come to be near their loved ones. But most come for the same reason immigrants have always flocked to this country—in search of meaningful work and a better life. The truth is that working-age immigrants (those who are fifteen to sixty-four years of age) are less likely than native-born Americans to receive government assistance. Immigrants have higher labor force participation rates than native-born Americans as well, with Hispanic men achieving an employment rate of 83.4 percent, compared with a 75 percent employment rate for non-Hispanic Whites.

Although we could lower welfare dependency among working-age immigrants even more by admitting more highly skilled immigrants, I fear that would also skew the immigrant pool in terms of countries of origin.

To their credit, Jack Kemp and Bill Bennett have tried, unsuccessfully, to caution the Right about attacking immigrants. Both were quite vocal in their opposition to California's Proposition 187 in 1994, saying that it would not solve the problem of illegal immigration but instead start a fight over limiting immigration, a fight that would eventually prove harmful to the Right.

Both men argued that the Right should instead focus on teaching American values to newcomers and keeping them off welfare.

While I'm not sure I necessarily want new Americans to be taught *all* of Bill Bennett's values, he and Kemp were certainly on target in urging their party to be more inclusive and less exclusive. The fact that the Right almost uniformly turned a deaf ear to their suggestion is telling.

What can we do to correct the flaws of our current immigration policy?

- We can change the system to one that favors skills, rather than the uniting of extended family.
- Stop illegal entry at the border.
- Deport illegal immigrants. But there is a wrong way and a right way. Let's not further restrict the legal

immigration route, causing even more to come to America any way they can.

- Tighten employer sanctions. The pro-business Right can't have it both ways. If they don't want illegal immigrants here, don't hire them as cheap labor. Those who do should be subject to punishment. Isn't it always about money?

Would America have been America without her immigrant peoples? U.S. immigration policy should be reviewed and reformed, but the debate doesn't have to be lopsided, hijacked, and dominated by the Right.

MULTICULTURALISM

Depending on who you ask, you'll get a thousand different definitions of what "multiculturalism" means. I feel it means an equal respect for all cultures; allowing each individual to determine the significance of his or her origins on one's present life and heritage.

In his book *The End of Racism,* Dinesh D'Souza tells us to rethink multiculturalism in a manner which I find patently offensive and fundamentally lacking.

Among D'Souza's claims:

- "Racism undoubtedly exists, but it no longer has the power to thwart Blacks or any other group in achieving their economic, political, and social aspirations."
- "America can become a multiracial society, but not a multicultural society."
- "No society can absorb unlimited diversity."

Like Martin Luther King, Jr., I believe that racism is *prejudice plus power*. It's one thing to harbor prejudicial views against a particular group of Americans; it's quite another to have the power and ability to act out one's discriminatory beliefs. The White Establishment still has the power to deny opportunity to persons of color simply because of the shade of their skin.

D'Souza claims that it is not racism that denies people of color entrance into selected colleges, access to rewarding jobs and professions, and the funds to successfully launch independent businesses. That is just plain false.

Right-wing conservatives like D'Souza point to a handful of Black Americans who have risen to national prominence, such as Colin Powell and Clarence Thomas, to prove their case. "If they can make it, why can't you?"

The truth is that both of these men *have* been discriminated against, but both have benefited from corrective programs like affirmative action. The only difference is that one will admit to it (General Powell) and the other won't.

D'Souza's belief that America can become a multiracial society but not a multicultural one is also wrong. We already are a multicultural society, although many want to deny this fact and turn back the clock. But I believe that people of different skin tones and cultural backgrounds can live under the same set of laws with a shared understanding of the rights and obligations of every other citizen.

D'Souza also claims that no society can absorb unlimited diversity. So what then is he suggesting as its limits? The fact is that there are no limits to diversity as long as equal respect and tolerance are accorded to all people, and all cultures. That's all it takes. It's really that simple.

D'Souza's book is nothing more than a waste of good trees. That so much bigoted, at times racist, and more often ignorant intellectual jargon can be passed off as quasiserious scholarship is a sad commentary on the fear of change that the Right has played to and helped to create.

The attack on multiculturalism is being launched on a number of fronts. Politicians and the public are starting to weigh in on the debate as well. Senator Bob Dole has called for eliminating bilingual education and courses aimed at "instilling ethnic pride." Dole has slammed individuals who have taken and benefited from these classes as the "embarrassed-to-be-American crowd."

Like Dorothy in *The Wizard of Oz,* Dole is still dazed that he's not in the Kansas of his childhood. He's obviously not aware that, in most major American cities, classes that teach English as a second language to foreign students and immigrants are overcrowded and long waiting lists are the norm. New immigrants to this country are trying to assimilate at a much faster pace than Dole or others are willing to recognize or admit.

I agree that all American citizens should be fluent in English. Our common language is part of the glue that holds us together. But multilingual education isn't a means of instilling "ethnic pride," nor is it a "therapy for low self-esteem." Bilingual education is simply a useful tool to get kids up to speed, especially at the elementary level.

California schools, home to roughly a third of the non-English-speaking schoolchildren in the nation, spend $400 million a year to teach 1.2 million children in languages other than English. The education of these kids would be immeasurably slowed if their teachers spoke to them at school in a language they didn't understand. How do we get immigrant kids to learn English if we don't first give them a way to tackle the classroom?

Who benefits or profits most from a bilingual society? Business and private enterprise. McDonald's, for example, can sell a lot more hamburgers when their employees can speak in more than one language. The same principle holds for airlines, retail outlets, and most service industries where the dollar is traded. Dole and the Right can complain all they want about bilingual education and push for an English-only society, but it doesn't take a rocket scientist to figure out that American free enterprise is the real winner.

The fear among conservative Republican voters that the so-called "American way of life" is being gradually undone is nonsense. This suggests that immigrants and American citizens of color cannot be boldly patriotic and at the same time proud of their respective cultures.

Many times on talk radio, I have found myself debating the concept of hyphenated Americans: African-Americans, Mexican-Americans, Asian-Americans. For some reason, those on the Right get bent out of shape when citizens of color refer to themselves in a "hyphenated way." The Right is bothered by the fact that such "Americans" place their cultural identity before their country. They also believe that hyphenated terminology is racially divisive, separating the country into various ethnic "camps." News flash! America was segregated long before the term African American ever surfaced.

I am an American and darn proud to be one. I'm also proud to be Black—not unlike Mexicans, Asians, and others who are proud of their heritage and their culture. Nobody seems to be bothered by the pride that Irish Americans so openly and boldly display. To suggest that because I refer to myself as an African American that I am somehow not patriotic is, well, unpatriotic. The two are not mutually exclusive.

In 1995, when the UCLA National Center for History proposed a set of voluntary guidelines for teaching history in primary and secondary schools, Dole and others on the Right widely criticized the guidelines, which were ultimately revised. But the debate caused by the furor over what to teach in U.S. history and how to teach it was one worth having. Many educators have a problem with the way U.S. history is taught because it is not infrequently inaccurate, unfair, and selective in the history it records. That is why there is such a need for programs and disciplines like Chicano and Black studies.

The Right believes that these distinct disciplines reimpose segregation in higher education. As a result, they have started their effort to "deracialize" these educational institutions and are also taking a hard look at government funding for historically Black colleges.

There is no good reason to set apart works by or about Blacks or others as long as they are not excluded from the regular curriculum. But too often that is not the case for Black or Chicano studies.

As long as predominantly White collegiate institutions, through their policies, practices, and curriculum—or the lack thereof—make students of color feel like unwanted guests, the need for culture disciplines will remain. Black colleges will continue to remain relevant as long as a smaller proportion of Black students graduate from integrated colleges (about 30 percent) than from all-Black or predominantly Black institutions.

For all the rhetoric from the Right about shutting down Black colleges, statistics show rather convincingly that Black students who graduate from Black colleges are hired into the labor market at a much faster and higher rate than Black students who attend predominantly White institutions. Isn't that what we want? A more educated Black populus, gainfully employed and contributing to America's tax base?

On college campuses across this country, multiculturalism and a healthy respect for diversity can and must be achieved. I would prefer to see the general curriculum at these schools changed to more accurately reflect the crises, conflicts, and contributions of all Americans. But until that happens, all attempts at multiculturalism are necessary alternatives.

America *is* both a multiracial and multicultural society. When both of these facts are acknowledged and appreciated by the nation and when that appreciation is evidenced through our policies, America will be far along its path to genuine equality.

NONUNANIMOUS JURY VERDICTS

There are any number of issues which the murder trial of O. J. Simpson raised for the American people—and indeed the world community—to ponder and discuss.

Race. Interracial relationships. Racism. Spousal abuse. Police misconduct. Jury reform. Television cameras in courtrooms. Morality. Family. Values. Safety and security. Judicial reform.

Another of the issues which I believe the Right is about to take on in their effort to "take back America"—given the length, expense, and circus atmosphere of the Simpson trial—is the matter of nonunanimous jury verdicts. Trials whereby a defendant can be convicted for any felony except murder—even if two of twelve jurors disagree. Presently, only two states use such a system: Oregon and Louisiana. The Supreme Court has upheld the Oregon system.

The unanimous jury system evolved from English common law over six hundred years ago and is so deeply ingrained in the American consciousness that we almost never consider that there are alternatives. At least not seriously. Until now.

The nonunanimous jury verdicts represent the easy way out, perhaps the path of least resistance at a time when many Americans are frustrated with a jury system that sometimes gets snagged by hung juries.

Proponents argue that the present unanimous jury requirement allows one or two jurors to frustrate the majority. On the flip side, however, a nonunanimous verdict would allow a majority to return swift decisions without the serious and prolonged deliberations that are usually required.

I don't agree that jurors are pressured into a unanimous verdict because they are tired of being in court, want to go home, or simply give up. Especially not after they have spent an inordinate amount of time listening to evidence from both sides. I think they understand their civic duty and work to reach a decision and bring the case to its dutiful conclusion.

On balance, prosecutors and court administrators love the nonunanimous jury system, saying there are far fewer hung juries and far more people convicted and sentenced to prison. Most judges seem to like it, too, arguing that it is a system that metes out justice fairly without compromising defendants' rights.

Conversely, many defense lawyers hate it for the most obvious reason. Less jurors needed to convict means a greater chance their clients will be found guilty, perhaps wrongfully. Timothy Allan Hinkhouse, twenty-four, says of Oregon's nonunanimous jury system, "It's not right. It's not fair." Hinkhouse was sentenced to seventy years for attempted murder, despite the fact that one juror obstinately refused to convict him. "It keeps Oregon's largest business going, which is the prison system."

Nonunanimous juries do appear to significantly reduce the number of hung juries. When the Oregon law was challenged in 1971, states requiring unanimous verdicts had hung jury rates of 5.6 percent in felony trials, nearly double the 3.1 percent rate for states with nonunanimous jury verdicts, according to Oregon's then-Solicitor General Jacob Tanzer.

Some studies suggest that, because jurors do not have to reach consensus, they don't deliberate as long or as thoughtfully. Yet Tanzer argued in *The Los Angeles Times* that: "The beauty of our system is that it [keeps] the one crackpot, the one person that would never see things the way others do, from holding up the entire system of justice." USC law professor Erwin Chemerinsky concurs. Referencing the Simpson case prior to its outcome, the educator said, "All you need is one person not willing to convict because of his [Simpson's] popularity and this case ends up with a hung jury. There is enormous tolerance for idiosyncratic behavior because we don't want to exclude the one angry man."

The "one crackpot" and "one angry man" statements by Tanzer and Chemerinsky highlight one of the primary reasons I'm opposed to nonunanimous jury verdicts. Their comments explain why the idea of lowering the level of proof will so appeal to the Right, who want convictions at any price. To label persons who happen to disagree with their jury colleagues as "crackpots" or "angry" social rebels shows a certain bias—and a presumption of guilt—which I believe the nonunanimous jury verdicts foster.

Former Los Angeles County District Attorney Robert Philibosian tried more than a decade ago to get nonunanimous juries approved by the state legislature. And the present district attorney, Gil Garcetti, has said that nonunanimous jury verdicts are "something that we have to look at."

Why? Because the D.A.'s office in L.A. County has

been stung by embarrassing losses in any number of high-profile cases (the first Menendez brothers' trial and the Rodney King trial). Yet their overall conviction rate is in the 90th percentile, not unlike most D.A.'s offices around the country—which is a pretty darn good conviction rate.

What's driving this prosecution-friendly, nonunanimous jury wagon is a win-at-all-costs mentality. Never mind a person's right to a fair trial or the presumption of innocence until proven guilty. Just win, baby.

I'm not persuaded that convincing twelve people of one's innocence or guilt is that difficult in most cases where the evidence is conclusive. Perhaps not being able to convince twelve jurors of a defendant's guilt beyond a reasonable doubt suggests that something is wrong with the case—not the jury.

My fear is that, around the country, those on the Left who work in the area of law enforcement will begin to yield to conservative voters who want to make it easier to convict defendants. The tragedy is that, once again, we will be catering to an agenda that we have allowed the Right to define. As Yogi Berra has said, "It will be déjà vu all over again."

I am very reluctant to lower the level of proof required by law to convict defendants just because it plays well in political circles. For me, it is an issue of fundamental fairness.

By lowering the level of proof needed for a conviction through nonunanimous jury verdicts, we risk locking up innocent people. No one wants the guilty to go free. But never should the innocent lose their liberty.

The system may not be perfect, but it still works better than any other in the world.

I believe that, before we so radically alter the way our system of jurisprudence has operated for hundreds of years, we must first challenge and *support* law enforcement and other investigatory agencies to do a better job of making their cases stick in court. Additionally, we must have truth in sentencing. If you do the crime, you will do the time.

No shortcuts.

DATA FLOW

After the German state prosecutor's office charged them with violating the country's pornography laws in December of 1995, CompuServe, the world's second-largest on-line service, was forced to block access to more than two hundred discussion groups on the Internet, many of which dealt with sexually explicit material. The German government argued that the company was obligated to use every technical resource available to it to block what the ultraconservative German government felt was illegal pornographic material.

Here in America, the United States Congress has already voted to stop the flow of "indecent" computer files into the country and has now turned its attention to restricting pornography, hate speech, and other offensive material on the Internet. Not an easy task when you consider that the content on any given Internet site can change daily.

My concerns with a Right-controlled Congress being

spurred on by the Christian Coalition to legislate what may or may not appear on the Internet are probably pretty clear by now. The Right's penchant for mandating what is good and what is bad for America frightens me at times. Most of us would agree that children should not be exposed to the obscene and offensive material found on certain Internet sites. I think we would also agree, however, that parents should take responsibility for what their children get exposed to on the global computer network. Indeed, there is a growing number of clickable icons on the Internet that serve as links to help parents access the tools they need to enforce whatever standards of morality they have set for their children.

Without question, the computer industry must be challenged to a higher standard of corporate responsibility as well. But I have always believed that selective viewing and selective purchasing are the best ways to boycott objectionable material, rather than allowing the Right to infringe upon the sacred privileges guaranteed by the First Amendment.

We must keep a close eye on abuse of the Internet and ward against hate speech and other material that no American with a conscience could embrace. The other eye must be kept on the Right to make sure that they don't start to control the data flow.

9

Leadership

Ironically, I find myself ending this book right where it began, talking about leadership. "Leaders," says noted author and USC professor Warren Bennis, "are people who are able to express themselves fully. They know who they are, what their strengths and weaknesses are, and how to fully deploy their strengths and compensate for their weaknesses. They also know what they want, why they want it, and how to communicate what they want to others in order to gain their cooperation and support. Finally, they know how to achieve their goals."

Time magazine, in the issue that named me as one of America's most promising leaders of the future, went on to say that: "America has become vastly suspicious of leaders." *Time* then asked the question: "[Does] the nation have any leaders left, especially young ones with promise and enthusiasm?"

Absolutely.

The question, it seems to me, is not whether we are still producing leaders in America, but whether Americans have developed an aversion to being led? My sense is that Americans, little by little, have become less trusting and more skeptical of our leaders—and not just our political leaders.

Maybe a little suspicion of leadership is a healthy thing. Certainly, several of our nation's worst mistakes were exacerbated by our disinclination to challenge government policy. It is not surprising that it was during the one sustained protest to the government in the sixties that the phrase **"Question authority"** was coined. Perhaps part of the aftermath of the Vietnam war was a deep-rooted sense of disillusionment with the government and politics.

Nonetheless, the convergence of America's growing lack of confidence in leaders, and our desperate need for them, necessitated by more complex political, social, and economic challenges both at home and abroad, is nothing short of frightening.

While many Americans may not want to be *led,* they do want to be *liberated* from the economic, political, and social shackles that we as a nation find ourselves in today. Many of these problems seem intractable. Now, more than ever, we need strong leaders with values and vision.

As Professor Bennis puts it: "We cannot function without leaders. Our quality of life depends on the quality of our leaders."

I have spent a great deal of time in this book questioning our leadership—or the lack thereof in this country. And, although most of my frustration, discontent, and consternation has been focused on the Right, I have not been shy about criticizing the Left as well. The Right, to my mind, wants to set the rules, not play by them, and later change them as often as necessary to maintain an unfair advantage for their angry, fearful, often privileged constituency. The Left, on the other hand, refuses to acknowledge that the road they've been driving us down is full of potholes. As I said earlier, insanity is doing the same thing the same way and expecting a different result. I don't believe that Americans today uniformly or arbitrarily reject *all* leaders; they do demand, however, that our leaders prove themselves competent to do the job.

The country's fixation in the fall of 1995 with whether or not General Colin Powell would make a run for the White House in 1996 had primarily to do with America's search for a competent leader. Never mind that, despite all the media hype, practically none of us—including General Powell—had a clue of *where* he might want to lead us. All along, I hoped that General Powell wouldn't be sucked in by the hype and base his decision about whether or not to enter the race on opinion or popularity polls.

After all, the same bored presidential press corps

that treated Powell with kid gloves and hung on his every utterance in the fall of 1995 would come to life in 1996 like an attack dog, looking for any issue to tear him apart.

In addition, it's one thing for a pollster to ask who *will* vote for Colin Powell; it's another thing for someone to actually vote for him in the election. For many in mainstream America, Colin Powell was a prototype of the kind of Black candidate they *could* support *if* they were to vote for a Black American seeking the highest office in the land. Little more. I found it rather interesting that, prior to the verdict in the O. J. Simpson case and Louis Farrakhan's Million Man March in Washington, General Powell was the potential Black presidential candidate who, for White America, transcended race. But had he not had the *right* responses to the media's questions about Simpson and Farrakhan, he no longer would have been the color-blind candidate.

Notwithstanding America's suspicion of modern-day leaders, America is still producing young leaders with "promise and enthusiasm" and the "requisite ambition, vision, and community spirit," as *Time* would have it, to rescue her future. And we will need them to solve the enormous problems which face this country.

Crime rates, taxes, and health care costs must come down. Education must improve. We must create better employment opportunities for all. The value of our dollar and our overall quality of life must be raised. I know it's much easier said than done. But the complex nature of these issues, and the willingness of self-interested politicians to keep borrowing against our future, must not deter us from fixing the problems.

After all, that's what leaders are for. To lead. To help shape the American frontier of tomorrow by serving as guides today.

In order to lead effectively in a new and vastly different world, I believe that we need a fundamentally different kind of leader. Here are some of the kinds of attributes I think we need in the leaders of tomorrow. I know that you can think of several more desirable qualities.

LEADERS WHO ARE PRACTICAL AND PROGRESSIVE

As I intimated earlier, if you ask most Americans about the major issues of our time, you're likely to get a short list that most anyone can agree to that includes abortion, affirmative action, crime, the environment, health care, race, national defense, the economy, and any of a dozen other items that shape the national agenda. But ask them how to solve the problems associated with these issues—or even which direction to go in—and we find raucous disagreement.

Some offer Republican solutions, some offer Democratic solutions, and others offer any number of solutions in between.

The fact is, no one political party or ideology has all the answers. As I indicated in Chapter 2, it has become increasingly clear that ideological labels like ''liberal'' and ''conservative'' are too narrow and simplistic for the complex array of problems confronting our nation.

I cannot remember when (or how) I became a liberal. I certainly never described or even thought of myself that way. Perhaps it was a process of elimination. Since no one who knows me would call me conservative, at least not in the way that term is commonly used today, I became a liberal by default. When I ran for City Council in 1990, somehow the "liberal" label stuck.

During the campaign, I realized how terribly restricting it could be to allow yourself and your politics to be defined by someone else. I kept trying to present my agenda one way, but the news media and my opponents kept painting me into a liberal box that I could not escape. I lost the race, of course, but walked away with a valuable lesson in the limitations of ideological labels.

We need the best **ideas,** not a precut **ideology,** and energy of all our people from the Right and the Left. We must recognize that most people are liberal on some issues and conservative on others. It's time to shape a new way of thought, a practical, progressive approach to moving us forward.

What do I mean by being practical and progressive? A practical progressive seeks practical approaches to problem-solving rather than strictly ideological ones. That means supporting the Left when it makes sense and challenging the Left when it fails to offer forward-looking solutions. It also means not being afraid to criticize our leaders and even our friends when they are wrong. One of the traps of being a "liberal" or "conservative" has been the fear of criticizing or offending anyone who shared the same ideological label.

Creating coalitions, supporting worthy people and causes across party or ideological lines, and telling the whole story are part of the nature of being a progressive. A progressive is not reactive, looking back endlessly at what was and trying to turn back the social and cultural clock. The world continues to evolve, and so must we. We cannot pretend the America of the turn of the century, or even midcentury, is the America of today. A progressive is proactive, seeking to take the parts of various social and political policies that work and trying to improve them.

That means advocating policies that will improve life for all Americans; policies that will seek to better the least among us and allow America to enjoy the fruits of all her vast humanity and diversity.

LEADERS WHO ARE UNAFRAID TO TAKE UNPOPULAR POSITIONS

When Abraham Lincoln refused to accede to the demands of the South, pushing the country into civil war, it was a dangerous and unpopular stance. When President Lyndon Johnson pushed 1964's historic Civil Rights Act through Congress, he had to outmaneuver Southern Democrats and conservatives, but it was the right thing to do. Harry Truman often said, "The buck stops here." That is the kind of leadership we need at the state and federal level today. Too few politicians are willing to vote their conscience and do the job they were elected to do in the first place. Now, more than ever, politicians read the public opinion polls, craft a piece of diluted compromise legislation, and pretend they are leading the nation. Some politicians seem to have only a constituency, not a conscience.

Their interest isn't so much enacting sound legislation that will help guide and improve the nation. Instead, they are more concerned with their own survival. They care more about reelection, and voting as safely as possible to satisfy the special interest groups and influence peddlers so that they can hold on to their seats. They are politicians but certainly not leaders. A leader is someone who does what is best for the country, whatever the fallout may be.

One of the reasons so many congressional Democrats lost in November 1994 is because they did the right thing and voted with their hearts on some key issues, such as the assault weapons ban and the Brady Bill. Their votes were largely unpopular in their home districts. Yet, they could not close their eyes to the fact that every day fifteen American children die from handgun violence. We have a gun epidemic in our country. We must get handguns and assault weapons off the streets. There's no legitimate reason for any law-abiding citizen to own an assault weapon. I don't care how much pressure the NRA applies, or how much money they spend, on this issue they are completely out of bounds and just plain wrong.

Many congressional Democrats voted for the ban. As a result, the Right and the NRA targeted these good men and women for defeat at the polls. These members of Congress knew they were putting their political lives on the line. But they voted against it, anyway. The fact is we *need* leaders who are willing to put their necks on the line sometimes. But if we abandon them on

Election Day, then we deserve the kind of fawning, re-active, poll-watching politicians we elect in their stead. The conservative circus in Washington and nationwide demands that we either put up or shut up. We cannot afford to lose the very leaders from the Left who are willing to buck the small-mindedness and special-interest-dominated policies of the Right.

The great American philosopher Ralph Waldo Emerson once said that listening to and trusting one's inner voice is what real leadership is all about.

Amen.

LEADERS WHO UNDERSTAND AND APPRECIATE DIVERSITY

When Bill Clinton pledged to make his Cabinet look more like America, he surprised many by making good on his promise once he was elected. He appointed more persons of color and women than any other President in history. His Administration truly did look more like today's America, unlike the other two branches of government: Congress and the Judiciary.

Clinton has shown himself to be one of the rare politicians who understands *and* appreciates diversity. Many of today's leaders have no interest in multiculturalism. They live in, work in, and represent a different kind of constituency.

Senator Bill Bradley is one of the only national lawmakers to speak often and eloquently about diversity and multiculturalism—and our lack of appreciation for it. Before going to the Senate, Bill Bradley spent ten years in the NBA playing for the New York

Knicks. He spent the majority of his time with Black players like Walt Frazier and Willis Reed; as a result, he came to understand and appreciate the Black experience, and see how Blacks and Whites could work together. The same, I believe, is true for Jack Kemp. As I noted earlier in this book, of all the members of the Republican party who were potential candidates for President in 1996, he was the one guy who genuinely spoke to all Americans. As the Secretary of Housing and Urban Development in the Bush Administration, Kemp got good marks from both conservatives and liberals, as well as the African American community. And Kemp was one of the few persons on the Right to speak out against the California anti-immigrant initiative in 1994. Because he understands and appreciates diversity. Like Bradley, his career began in professional sports, as quarterback for the Buffalo Bills. He worked side by side with Black men every day and took that experience with him to Washington. I'd hate to think that only former professional athletes can appreciate diversity.

One of my favorite local politicians was Kenneth Hahn, a former Los Angeles County supervisor, who served the community for forty-two years before retiring in 1992, when a stroke prevented him from seeking reelection. Hahn was a White man representing an overwhelmingly Black and Hispanic district. And he was invincible. No candidate of color who had the nerve to run against him even came close.

Why was he so successful? The answer is simple. Hahn understood and appreciated the ethnic diversity in his district. He listened and responded to his constituents, and that paid off for him at the polls, time and time again.

As our country has become more culturally and ethnically diverse, our national leadership has not adapted accordingly. What does Senator Jesse Helms know about diversity? What Black neighborhoods has Bob Dole visited lately? Most politicians on Capitol Hill live, work, and play in a White environment. They don't go out of their way to interact with, understand, or relate to a multicultural America. The closest they get to the Black experience is rubbing elbows with Clarence Thomas at a wine and cheese reception.

They're closing their eyes to the future, because the America of old, dominated by a White political machinery, is slowly but surely coming to an end. The America of today is a beautiful mosaic of different colors and ethnicities: White, Black, Latino, Asian, Persian, and so much more.

Though you'd never know it from hanging out on Capitol Hill.

What do we do? I can only hope that, as more of the old-line Right are voted out of office or retire, future leaders from younger generations, having grown up in the most integrated America ever, will be more open to working side by side with others.

LEADERS WHO THINK, "ONE TERM"

The reason nothing ever changes in Washington is because the people in Washington never change. No, this is not an argument for term limits. Elections are term limits. If we don't like the bums, we can throw 'em out.

But can you imagine what it would be like to have politicians who were more concerned about what they legislated rather than their strategy for reelection? True reformers who attacked their task with the full intention of serving only one term, cleaning up the mess, and then going back home. We might actually see some real change in Washington.

Politicians get elected on "outsider" and "anti-incumbent" platforms and then, once in office, turn their attention to organizing fund-raisers for their reelection campaigns. And who are the ones with the big bucks to contribute? Not you or I, but the rich special interests and PACs.

You know the story. Sadly, because of their dependency on the money for reelection, you and I, in little ways and big ways, get sold out.

In 1992, independent candidate Ross Perot pledged to serve one term only if elected President. I believe his promise was one reason voters were so fascinated with him. Perot was the wrong guy, but he had the right idea. It doesn't take a lifetime to clean up America's political mess, it only requires the concerted actions of brave men and women. It only takes good ideas based on good intentions, not extremist ideology.

Perhaps one day we'll actually have someone run for President on a one-term platform, and serve without one eye on the polls. Political pundits would quickly dismiss such an idea, arguing that the President would be a lame duck from Day One. Not if he or she had the full support of the American people who indeed want to stop the insanity. Especially at a time when our problems call for sometimes difficult and courageous decisions. We need an army of leaders willing to make those decisions, whatever the consequences.

LEADERS . . . NOT PREACHERS

People are tired of being *preached* to—from the Left and the Right. They're tired of being addressed as if they were schoolchildren.

A leader is someone with a vision for the country who expresses him or herself fully, sharing those ideas about the direction the country should be moving in, helping to fashion a consensus that can move us along the way.

We don't need political preachers who shout condemnation from the pulpit or podium down to us in the pews. People like Pat Robertson, Newt Gingrich, Jerry Falwell, Rush Limbaugh, Pat Buchanan, or Ralph Reed. It's their way—or no way. They hold all the solutions. Only *they* know what's best for the country. If we don't heed their admonitions, our souls and our nation will be consigned to perdition.

Republican presidential candidate Lamar Alexander even went as far as to tell true believers at a Christian Coalition convention that the next President should be a "little bit of a preacher." That is *not* what we need. The last thing America needs is the kind of isolationism and protectionism, intolerance and nativism the Right espouses. People are alarmed by the hype from the Christian Coalition. Were they to get their way, America would indeed become a scary place to live. Fortunately, sooner or later they always go overboard and frighten people off. Look at what happened in

1994 in Merrimack, New Hampshire, when the Christian Right got control of the school board using Christian Coalition leader Ralph Reed's game plan. As soon as the new members of the board proposed teaching "creation science" in the schools, parents got involved and stopped them dead in their tracks. More moderate voices prevailed in the next election.

The Christian Right, by its very intolerance, ends up creating nothing more than Christian Fright.

LEADERS WHO LEAD . . . NOT MANAGE

Too many of our so-called leaders today are not leaders at all but simply managers of our huge governmental bureaucracy. These politicians tend to come up with quick fixes instead of long-term solutions. Michael Dukakis was portrayed by the media as an able administrator—rather than a leader. The public, sensing the distinction, flatly rejected his presidential bid. Sadly, George Bush, his opponent, was hardly a visionary himself.

A political leader is one who has ideas to master social, economic, and political challenges, rather than surrendering to them. Professor Warren Bennis, in his classic leadership textbook *On Becoming a Leader,* defined the differences between a leader and a manager in the following ways:

- The manager administers; the leader innovates.
- The manager maintains; the leader develops.
- The manager asks how and when; the leader asks what and why.

- The manager accepts the status quo; the leader challenges it.
- The manager does things right; the leader does the right thing.

The problems and issues which confront this country today are so difficult and potentially threatening that we don't need to have them *managed,* we need to find a way to solve them. The 1990s demand leaders with original thoughts and long-term perspectives on problem-solving.

Unfortunately, too many of our politicians seem to be looking for a way to manage the mess. We need someone to clean it up.

LEADERS WHO ARE PEOPLE-FRIENDLY

Too many politicians these days are less interested in our citizens than they are in lobbyists, PACs, and other interest groups. Some members of Congress rarely go back and visit their home districts! They seem less focused on passing "people-friendly" legislation than in creating or dismantling institutions, systems, and structures.

"We have a system in Washington," said former Common Cause president Fred Wertheimer, "where members of Congress have their professional lives paid for by the very people who are trying to influence their decisions. They have in many cases their personal lives subsidized by lobbyists and special-interest groups who pay for their vacation trips, their entertainment, their Super Bowl tickets. That's a corrupting system, and that engulfs everyone in it because the whole system breaks down.''

In explaining the situation to National Public Radio, Wertheimer said that the people who put up the money have a lot more influence than everyday citizens. He used the issue of health care reform to make his point. "The industries involved put up an enormous amount of money and have been for years," he said. "And the fact of the matter is, we don't have health care reform."

That's not people-friendly politics, and that has got to change.

LEADERS WHO ARE SERIOUS ABOUT CAMPAIGN FINANCE REFORM

Every politician from the Right and the Left agrees that we must have campaign finance reform. I've heard it a thousand times. But so far it's been all talk and no action. Money is still the mother's milk of politics, more so today than ever before.

There is something very wrong with our system when a multimillionaire like Republican Michael Huffington can spend $30 million—albeit his own money—in an attempt to buy himself a California Senate seat. The expected November 1996 Massachusetts U.S. Senate race between incumbent Democratic Senator John Kerry and popular Republican Governor William Weld may prove to be the costliest Senate race in history. Such financing restricts top state and federal offices to the wealthy and incumbents, who generally have little trouble raising money from lobbyists, corporations, PAC funds, and wealthy constituents.

Republicans Dan Quayle, Bill Bennett, and Jack Kemp decided not to run for President in 1996 for one simple reason: It was just too expensive. Is it any wonder we're not attracting the best and the brightest political leaders? They can't afford to be a part of the process. We can't afford to have a governmental system run almost exclusively by the rich.

The overriding influence of money must be taken out of politics. There has to be a better way. We need to enact and enforce strict campaign spending limits, legislate free television time for all qualified candidates, and offer additional federal matching funds. Our political leaders must be elected on the basis of their ideas, not the bounty of their income.

The Republican freshmen now in Congress were elected in 1994 on a platform of term limits, radical change, and giving government back to the people. From the moment they arrived, they began backtracking and making plans to overstay their welcome. Term limits was the first "principle" to go by the boards. According to *The Wall Street Journal,* the seventy-three freshman GOP lawmakers raised money "more aggressively" than any other new Congress, pulling in donations that were 34 percent higher than their predecessors.

I rarely agree with Pat Buchanan on anything, but I am in favor of his proposed campaign finance reforms. Buchanan called for an end to corporate campaign contributions and a ban on senators collecting campaign funds from outside their states. House members would be prohibited from accepting campaign donations from outside their congressional districts. I feel that anything we can do to reform the process—whether it comes from Ted Kennedy or Pat Buchanan—is a step in the right direction.

There are other good ideas that have surfaced in recent years. Florida passed a law in 1991 that puts a cap on total spending limits for state campaigns that receive partial public financing. Arizona, Kentucky, Missouri, New Jersey, Oregon, and Montana passed similar laws and the eyes of both parties are focused on California and Maine, where 1996 initiatives calling for full public funding of state campaigns may be put before the voters. If passed, the days of a wealthy unknown almost beating a popular incumbent, simply because of a $30 million war chest, would be history. And indeed, the huge financial advantage incumbents enjoy over virtually any newcomer would be lessened, and the playing field largely leveled.

And it's about time. A democracy should be about earning votes, not jockeying for purse strings, about campaigning on the issues, not concocting the right political "spin." Let's all work to give America back to those to whom it belongs—"We the People."

About the Author

Tavis Smiley, thirty years old, is a nationally known television and radio commentator and was previously a top aide to former Los Angeles Mayor Tom Bradley. Selected by *Time* magazine as one of the nation's fifty top future leaders, he has been a featured analyst on CNN, CNBC, "Geraldo," "Entertainment Tonight," and many other shows. He lives in Los Angeles.